Mangled English

Gervase Phinn

illustrated by Matthew Phinn

Dalesman

First published in 2013 by Dalesman
an imprint of
Country Publications Ltd
The Water Mill, Broughton Hall
Skipton, North Yorkshire BD23 3AG
www.dalesman.co.uk

Paperback edition published in 2014

Text © Gervase Phinn 2013
Illustrations © Matthew Phinn 2013

ISBN 978-1-85568-337-2

Printed in China on behalf of Latitude Press Ltd.

The quotation on page 58 from *A Boy's Own Dale: A 1950s Childhood
in the Yorkshire Dales* by Terry Wilson, published by Ebury Press, is
reprinted by permission of the Random House Group Limited.

Dedication
For the two English teachers who gave me a love of the English language:
Ken Pike and Mary Wainwright.

CONTENTS

FOREWORD

I was warned by a friend that when visiting Barcelona with my wife we should be especially careful for there were a great many pickpockets about. It was a good idea, we were advised, to secrete money and credit cards on our person in a body belt. In town I went into a shop which sold cases and said to the lugubrious-faced man behind the counter:

"I'd like a body bag for my wife."

"Wouldn't we all," he replied, smiling wryly.

I am sure that many of my readers will have done something similar: said the wrong thing and in doing so caused some amusement. Unless one happens to be Winston Churchill or Professor David Crystal, there but for the grace of God go we all.

This book is not an academic text on language or a grammar book or a guide to the use of correct punctuation. It is a light-hearted look at the mishandling of this rich and powerful language of ours. It is about the things we say and write which can cause unintentional humour.

I should like to thank those who, in their misuse of English, have unwittingly contributed to this book. I should also like to thank my son Matthew Phinn for the splendid illustrations; Robert Flanagan, Managing Director of Country Publications, for his continued support and encouragement; Linda McFadzean, my publicist, for her sterling efforts on my behalf; and my ever-patient editor and friend Mark Whitley.

Gervase Phinn

INTRODUCTION

"A man that seeketh precise truth, had need to remember what every name he uses stands for; and to place it accordingly; or else he will find himself entangled in words, as a bird in lime-twigs; the more he struggles, the more be-limed."
(Hobbes's *Leviathan*)

Robert McClosky, a US State Department spokesman, once said:
  "I know you believe that you understand what you think I said, but I am not sure that you recognise that what you heard is necessarily what I meant."

How true. What we say and write can lead to a great deal of misunderstanding and unintentional mirth. "Better to trip with the feet than with the tongue," said Zeno 300 years before the birth of Jesus Christ. Shakespeare, that master wordsmith, shows us in his plays that words can be delightful and amusing but also can be cruel, cutting and dangerous in their seduction.

English is the most widespread language in the world, with a billion people speaking it. Five hundred million people use English as their mother tongue, and it is the native language of twelve nations and the official or semi-official language of thirty-three countries.

Of the world's 2,700 languages, English is arguably the richest in vocabulary and certainty ranks as one of the most demanding to master. The *Oxford English Dictionary* records nearly a million words and adds three hundred new ones every year. The average English-speaking person uses only about two thousand words in his or her vocabulary. The more educated use twice that.

English is a rich and poetic language, but is more complex, irregular and eccentric than most other written languages, and is arguably the most difficult European language to read and write. This is what makes it so fascinating.

Beset with pitfalls, colloquialisms, jargon, sloppy vulgarisms, slang, faulty grammar, misplaced apostrophes, dangling participles, split infinitives, misspellings, double negatives and euphemisms, the English language offers a rich seam for a book which looks at just how tricky and troublesome, idiosyncratic and illogical, ambiguous and arduous it can be.

"IT'S A BOOK ABOUT SCHOOLS BY THE MAN WITH THE FUNNY NAME"

Bookshop 'asked-fors'

I am sure I owe some of the success of my stories and poems to the fact that I have such an unusual name. One customer at the White Rose Bookshop in Thirsk, North Yorkshire, asked Sue, the proprietor, for "that book about schools by the man with the funny name". She immediately reached for my latest novel.

Of course booksellers are so adept at finding certain books from the scant information given by customers to fulfil their requests, sometimes known in the trade as an 'asked-for'.

On Independent Booksellers' Day I manned the counter at the Grove Bookshop in Ilkley. This is the third occasion I have acted as the shop assistant in a bookshop and each time I have received requests for some most unusual books.

There was the man who asked for a copy of 'Park Y'. I informed him that I had never heard of it. Neither had the manager of the shop. "It's by the famous Yorkshire interviewer," the customer told me. I gathered he was referring to Michael Parkinson and managed to locate a copy of his autobiography, *Parky*.

Then I was asked by another would be book-buyer, "Who wrote The Diary of Anne Frank?"

Another requested "a dinosaur book with real photographs in it".

A fourth customer asked for a copy of "*Hamlet* the novel in proper English and not the play version".

A grandmother asked for a copy of the book her granddaughter was reading at school. "It's called 'Hardy Drew and the Nancy Boys'," she told me. I managed to find her a copy of *Nancy Drew and the Hardy Boys*.

One customer in my local bookshop asked the manager if she could tell her the title of the book featured on the Richard and Judy television programme.

"I don't know the author or the title," she said, "but it's got a green cover and it's about so big."

Here are a few other genuine asked-fors in bookshops:

'The Great Gas Bill' by Scott Fitzgerald.

'The Adventures of Huckleberry Hound' by Mark Twain.

'Civilization and its Discotheques' by Sigmund Freud.

'The Girl with the Dragon and the Baboon' by Stieg Larsson.

'Colour Me Purple' by Alice Walker.

'Harry Potter and the Chamberpot Secret' by J K Rowling.

'Satanic Nurses' by Salman Rushdie.

'Tess of the Dormobiles' by Thomas Hardy.

'The Canine Mutiny' by Herman Wouk.

'The Lion in the Wardrobe' by C S Lewis.

'Lionel Richie and his Wardrobe' by Cecily Lewis.

Less Miserable.

"Do you have a copy of 'The Great Gas Bill'
by Scott Fitzgerald?"

'Tequila Mockingbird' by Harper Lee.

'Angel Dust' by Frank McCourt.

'Lord of the Files' by William Golding.

'She Stoops to Conga' by Oliver Goldsmith.

'Handwriting for the Television.'

'Major Morelli's Violin' by Louis de Bernieres.

'The Dinosaur Cookbook' (The Dinah Shore Cookbook).

James Joyce's 'Useless'.

The Communist Man's a Fatso

'Death in Denial' by Agatha Christie.

'Donkey Oats' by Miguel de Cervantes.

'Catch Her in the Eye' by J D Salinger.

'Hard Luck' by Charles Dickens.

'Good Times' by Charles Dickens.

'Olive or Twist' by Charles Dickens.

'The Brothers Carry Them Off' by Fyodor Dostoyevsky.

'Ann, Karen and Edna' by Leo Tolstoy.

'Ann in Spectacles' by J B Priestley.

'The Odd Sea' by Homer.

'Twenty Kinds of Blue' by 'some woman'.

MEMOIRS OF A JAPANESE CHICKEN SEXER

Unusual book titles

Publishers, like their authors, try and come up with eye-catching titles, those which will be imaginative, intriguing, appropriate and original.

Some books which appeared in the nineteenth century, such as *Flashes from the Welsh Pulpit* by J Gwnora Davies (ed), published in 1889 by Hodder & Stoughton, or *Vince the Rebel; or, Sanctuary in the Bog* by G Manville Fenn, published by Chambers in 1897, would, I guess, not have sounded particularly noteworthy at the time; the double-entendres are clearly unintentional.

One wonders, however, about others which have been published more recently, such as *The Big Book of Busts* (1994) by John L Watson and *Women on the Job* (1979) by Judith Buber Agassi. Are the authors, as Geoff, my Cockney window cleaner might observe, "'avin' a larf?".

The Bookseller, the British publishing industry's trade journal, regularly amuses readers with examples of the most bizarre book titles and awards the Diagram Book Prize for the weirdest of the year. Well, you can't get more bizarre than these genuinely published books:

Memoirs of a Japanese Chicken Sexer in 1930s Hebden Bridge

"Look, Daddy, I found this book – is it yours?
It's called 'The Big Problems of Small Organs'."

The Romance of Leprosy

The Sunny Side of Bereavement, by Rev Charles E Cooledge

Fishing for Boys, by J H Elliott

Handbook for the Limbless

Tinklings from the Sheepfolds

Leadership Secrets of Attila the Hun

Exposure and Removal of the Brain

Old Age: Its Cause and Prevention

Goblinproofing One's Chicken Coop

Wife Battering: A Systems Theory Approach

Exercise in the Bath

How Tea Cosies Changed the World

Aeroplane Designing for Amateurs

Greek Rural Postmen and Their Cancellation Numbers

Highlights in the History of Concrete

Proceedings of the Second International Workshop on Nude Mice

Erections on Allotments

Eternal Wind

Queer Doings in the Navy

Scouts in Bondage

The Big Problems of Small Organs

The Care and Feeding of Stuffed Animals

How to Sharpen Pencils

Cooking with Poo

Last Chance at Love — Terminal Romances

The Complete Suicide Manual

Scurvy Past and Present

Organising Deviance

Butchering Livestock at Home

Bombproof Your Horse

Picture Your Dog in Needlework

A Do-It-Yourself Submachine Gun

Knife Throwing: A Practical Guide

Rope Spinning
The Art of Faking Exhibition Poultry
The Secret Art of Chinese Leg Manoeuvres
The Walking Stick Art of Self-Defence
    by 'An Officer in the Indian Police'
Invisible Dick
A French Letter Writing Guide
Girls on the Pansy Patrol
Under Two Queens
Who's Who in Cocker Spaniels

One of the set texts my son Richard had to study when he was training to be a chartered accountant was the ambiguously titled reference book *The Accountants' Handbook of Fraud and Commercial Crime*.

When my daughter was a baby we visited an eye specialist. In his consulting room I glanced across the various books on the shelf and discovered *Cataract Extraction Through the Back Passage*. I determined that, should I ever need to have my cataracts removed, I would stay well away from this particular surgeon.

"I'M CALLED CARLSBERG — IT'S MY DAD'S FAVOURITE DRINK"

What's in a name?

When I was a lad growing up in Rotherham in the 1950s there were Jimmys and Terrys, Michaels and Ronalds, Martins and Kevins, but Gervases, you might be surprised to learn, were somewhat rare. Now, of course, children are given the most unusual, not to say bizarre names. Brooklyn Beckham, Peaches Geldof and the other children of the rich and famous are not alone in their unusual appellations. But I have yet to meet a child in a school called Gervase.

It is a fact that, wherever I go, I have to either repeat or explain this unusual name of mine. I have got quite accustomed to this by now and have come to expect that it will inevitably be misspelt or mispronounced. Over my years in teaching I collected a delightful range of inventive guesses which appeared on my letters. They ranged from 'Grievous Pain' to 'Gracious Dhin'. I have been called 'Germane', 'Germain', 'Germinal', 'Gercase', 'Gerund', 'Gervarse' and even 'Geraffe'. My surname has appeared as 'Flynn', 'Finn', 'Thin', 'Tinn', 'Pinn' and 'Chinn'.

My favourite appeared when I was in my first year of teaching. A letter arrived addressed to 'Mr Phunn, Master-in-Charge of Games'. "All Phunn and Games, eh, Gervase?", the head teacher had remarked drily as he passed me the letter.

I once received a delightful letter from a new father who informed me that his wife had given birth to a healthy boy. The baby was overdue but the mother-to-be was against having an epidural. The doctor informed her that, should the baby not arrive before the following morning, then it would have to be induced.

The nurse, seeing the woman was feeling low, gave her one of my books to cheer her up. One particular anecdote made her laugh so much it brought on the baby. The proud father said he and his wife were so grateful that the child had been born without being induced. He thanked me for my part. I replied, asking him if they had decided to name the child after me.

"We're not that grateful," he told me.

The Office of National Statistics shows that there has been a real decline in names like Edna, Ethel, Irene, Ada and Olive for girls; and Norman, Walter, Percy, Herbert and Harold for boys. The most popular names now are Jack, Harry, Thomas and Oliver for boys and Grace, Emma and Olivia for girls.

Recent research suggests that many traditional names are in danger of dying out. In 1907 Gertrude was very popular but not one baby was given that name last year. The modern trend is for parents to name their babies after celebrities (Keira, Demi, Britney, Kristen, Sylvester) or give them invented names (Tolly, Canter, Missy, Cobert).

Some parents take it into their heads to call their children all sorts of weird and wonderful names. Fine biblical names like Hannah and Bartholomew are rarely heard these days. Instead, a growing number of children are named after the offspring of pop singers, film stars, footballers and celebrities. There's Romeo Beckham and Prince Jackson, Satchel Allen and Zowie Bowie, Sage Moonbled Stallone and Moxie Crimefighter Gillette (the daughter of magician Penn Gillette, of Penn & Teller).

One child very nearly went through life with the exotic name of Onacardie. The vicar asked the parents at the christening:

"And what do you name this child?"

The mother replied loudly, "Onacardie".

The vicar had just begun sprinkling the water over the baby's head and intoning "I christen this child Onacardie…" — only to be quickly interrupted by the irate mother.

"No, no, vicar!" she hissed. "On 'er cardy. The name's written on her cardigan. We want her to be called Siobhan."

Speaking of christenings, I was recently told the following tale about a Methodist minister conducting a baptismal service in the Yorkshire Dales, who asked the father, a farm labourer by trade, the name of the child to be christened. The proud father announced that the name was Homer. One should never judge people by their appearances, thought the minister. Here was a man of some erudition who was clearly a great admirer of the classical scholar.

"Homer was a great philosopher," the minister told the father after the service. "I too share your interest in the classics."

"Eh?" asked the father.

"Homer. The man after whom you named your baby son."

"Nay, vicar," replied the father, "it's nowt to do wi' that. I keeps pigeons."

When I undertook a school inspection I would trawl through the registers to note absences and came across names more unusual than my own. The ones listed below have been supplemented by those told to me by teachers — all, I assure you, are genuine.

> **Boys' names:**
> Aztec Smith
> Adrian Wall (with a father called Walter Wall)
> Duncan Biscuit
> Ignatius Spratt and Jack Spratt (twins)

Mark King
Maximus Maxwell
Tristan Thistle
Mitchell Lynn
Justin Finnerty
Seymour Legg
Sean Head
Tim Burr
Phil Hole
Gerry Attick

Girls' names:
Eileen Dover
Sandi Beech
Summer Day
Noleen Mutton
Emerald Stone
Teresa Green
Nora Bone
Dee Zaster
Ima Kettle
Rosemary Border
Hazel Nutt
Daisy Chain
Daisy Roots
Penny Wise
Terri Bull
Anne Teak
Sue Ridge

Over the years as a school inspector I collected quite a list. I've met Barbie, Kristofer, Buzz, Curston, Mykell, Charleen, Kaylee, Scarlet, Egypt, Heyleigh, Jordana, Blasé (pronounced Blaze), Gooey (spelt Guy), a child whose surname was Pipe and a first

"Are you quite sure you want your daughter christened Anne, Mr and Mrs Teak?"

name Duane, and a child called Portia but spelt Porsche for, as the teacher explained to me with a wry smile, the girl's father had always wanted a Porsche car.

I've come across Mimi, Dayle, Shalott (pronounced Charlotte), Precious, Roxanne, Tiggy, Trixie, Terri, the twins Holly and Hazel Wood, Cheyenne, Billi-Jo, Tammy-Lou and a boy named Gilly.

In one school there were two sets of twins from the same family, aged ten and eleven respectively, named after great tragic heroines: Cleopatra and Cassandra, Desdemona and Dido. A girl called Brontë had a younger brother named Steinbeck. Then there were the brother and sister, Sam and Ella, which, when said at speed, sounded like food poisoning.

A head teacher told me once she taught three sisters called Paris Smout, Vienna Smout, Seville Smout.

"It is just as well," she told me, "that her parents didn't go on a romantic city-break to Brussels."

In one infant school in Bradford I came across a large girl with a plump face, frizzy hair in huge bunches and great wide eyes.

"What's your name?" I asked the child.

"Tequila," she replied. "I'm named after a drink."

"Tequila Sunrise," I murmured.

"No," pouted the child. "Tequila Braithwaite."

I was told by the head teacher of a Catholic school that it was the practice in the church for children to be named after saints and he was at school with a boy called Innocent, a name adopted by a number of popes.

"I suppose it must have been difficult having to live up to the name Innocent," I observed.

"It certainly was," he replied, "and something of a cross to bear. His second name was Bystander."

"I have a pet theory about first names," another head teacher told me. "Over the many years I have been in education I have come to the conclusion that Shakespeare got it wrong when he said 'What's in a name? That which we call a rose by any other name would smell as sweet.' I learned very early on that boys called Richard tend to be well-behaved, quiet children who work hard, Matthews are very polite and thoughtful, Dominics are little charmers, Damiens have far too much to say for themselves and Kevins are accident-prone. Penelopes tend to be lively and interested, Jennys tend to be sporty, Traceys too big for their boots and Elizabeths little darlings."

A survey by School Stickers examined the names of over 60,000 children who logged good behaviour awards on online sticker books. It found that boys called Benjamin, Alex, Mohammed and Aaron were the most likely to be the best behaved children. For girls Elisabeth, Rosie, Grace and Emma featured highly on the good-behaviour list. The boys' names which appeared least were Bradley and Jacob for boys, and Paige and Phoebe for girls.

"And what is your name?" asked the teacher of the infant.
    "Alex."
    "Alex what?"
    "....ander," replied the child.

Like the head teacher I tend to disagree with Shakespeare and go along with Oscar Wilde, who said that "names are everything".

A teacher at a West Yorkshire school was pointing out that a surname often indicated the trade of the ancestors of those who bore the name. He gave, as example, Smith, Taylor, Baker and others. Then he questioned one of the boys.
    "What were your ancestors, Webb?"
    "Spiders, sir."

The twentieth century was arguably the Age of the Pseudonym, especially in the worlds of the cinema and pop music. I wonder if the likes of Woody Allen (Allan Stewart Konigsberg), Fred Astaire (Frederick Austerlitz), Lauren Bacall (Betty Joan Perske), Dirk Bogarde (Derek van den Bogaerde), Richard Burton (Richard Jenkins), Michael Caine (Maurice Micklewhite), Joan Crawford (Lucille Le Sueur), Tony Curtis (Bernard Schwartz), Kirk Douglas (Issur Demsky) and Cary Grant (Alexander Leach) would have made it to the silver screen with their original names?

Pop stars and rock singers (or their agents or managers) more than any want a name to set the singer apart, a name to remember — Englebert Humperdinck (Arnold George Dorsey), Madonna (Madonna Louise Ciccone), Elton John (Reginald Dwight), Lulu (Marie Lawrie), Alice Cooper (Vincent Furnier), Chubby Checker (Ernest Evans).

When I was growing up, the male pop stars had short, solid, manly names: Cliff Richard, Tommy Steele, Jess Conrad, Adam Faith, Marty Wilde, Billy Fury, P J Proby, Tom Jones. In the 1970s and '80s, when I was teaching, quite a number of boys arrived in my classroom named after their mothers' favourite singers.

I read with some amusement about the riot at a christening occasioned by the irate grandfather, an old soldier, when he learnt that his first grandchild was to have the middle name of Adolf.

Authors' names are sometimes very appropriate to the topics of their books:

> *Machine Tool Operation* by Aaron Axelrod
> *Punishment* by Robin Banks
> *Sex Education* by Mary Breasted
> *Fruit Growing Outdoors* by Raymond Bush
> *The Boys' Own Aquarium* by Frank Finn
> *The Illustrated History of Gymnastics* by John Goodbody

The Encyclopaedia of Association Football by Maurice Golesworthy
The Grace of God by A Lord
Electronics for Schools by R A Sparkes
Put it in Writing by David Blot

I once undertook a school inspection, and on the team were Mr Phinn, Mr Pike, Mrs Gill and Mrs Roach. The head teacher ran his finger down the list of inspectors before remarking wryly, "Something a bit fishy here".

I have to admit to having a chuckle when I read about the hoax telephone calls to Dublin Zoo. It can't have been much fun for those receiving them.

"Good afternoon, Dublin Zoo. How may I help you?"

"I'm responding to an urgent call from Mr Rory Lion. If he's not available, Anna Conda will take the call."

"We have not lost our sense of humour," said the marketing manager, "but with the calls coming in at a rate of thirteen a minute it's no laughing matter."

In desperation she has recorded the following welcome message on the answerphone:

"If you are wanting to speak to a Mr Rory Lion, C Lion, G Raff, Ann T Lope or E Guana you are the victim of a hoax message."

This of course might cause something of a problem should Mr Don Kee or Mr Jack Rabbit be appointed to the zoo.

ALWAYS USE A SPILL CHUCKER

Problematic spellings

Aoccdring to rseerach at an Elingsh uinwevtisy, it deosn't mttaer in what order the ltteers in a word are pclaed, the olny iprmoatnt thing is that the frist and lsat ltteer is in the rghit pclae. The rset can be a total mses and yiou can still raed it wouthit porbelms. This is bcuseae we do nit raed ervey lteter by itelsf but the wrod as a wlohe.

The chairman of governors tut-tutted as he looked though the applications at the interview for the headship of the school.

"It's a great pity, Mr Phinn," he said, "that the standards of spelling have declined so much since I was at school."

He pointed to a letter of application in which the word 'liaison' had been spelt incorrectly.

"Even head teachers can't spell these days," he bemoaned.

"'Liaison' is a difficult word,' I said in the applicant's defence, "and I think you will agree that we all have problems with certain words at one time or another."

"Mr Phinn," said the chairman of governors pompously, "I don't have any difficulty. I pride myself on being a very good speller. I have no problem with spelling."

Well, bully for him, I thought, but I bet he does. He, like many

I have met who think they are excellent spellers, suffered from something of a delusion. I wonder how he would have coped with the following words:

embarrassed	desperate	separate
flotilla	symmetry	restaurateur
disparate	broccoli	benefited
census	calendar	innocuous
forgo	targeted	minuscule
instalment	keenness	battalion
tonsillitis	supersede	competent
withhold	occurred	innovate
incur	idiosyncrasy	filigree

None of us is a perfect speller and occasionally even the best of us has a problem. I was tempted to give him my 'little test' of thirty commonly used words which I have set on my English courses to teachers to demonstrate the loveable lunacies of the English spelling system. Or should that be 'lovable'? Or can it be both? You see what I mean?

George Bernard Shaw famously demonstrated the wild phonetic inconsistency of English by pointing out that, if English spelling were phonetically consistent, then the spelling of 'fish' might be 'ghoti': 'gh' as in 'laugh', 'o' as in 'women' and 'ti' as in 'station.'

If every word in English was spelt (or should that be 'spelled' or can it be both?) the way it sounds, it would be so much easier but this is not the case. One in ten words is not spelled the way it sounds and many of the non-phonic words are amongst those most frequently used in the language — words like 'the', 'of', 'one', 'two', 'could', 'shall', 'ought', 'woman', 'women', 'write' and 'people'. One could never solve the spelling of 'could' or 'thorough' by trying to relate their letters to the sounds.

I recall a clever child once asking me, "So why is the word 'phonics' not spelt the way it sounds?"

"Dear hoteliar, I am wryting to complane about my resent stay – I was definately embarassed by the seperate acomodation..."

Once in an infant school I came across a most inventive little speller who had written 'egog' at the top of the page.

"What does this say?" I enquired (or should that be 'inquired' or can it be both?).

"Can't you read?" she asked.

"I can," I replied, "but I am not sure about this word."

She sighed. "'edgehog," I was told.

In another school a child had written 'yrnetin' (wire netting) and another 'metantatipi' (meat and taty pie).

My former English master Mr Dyeball would give us a sentence each week which contained some tricky spellings, such as:

'Outside the cemetery an embarrassed pedlar liaised with a harassed cobbler who was gauging the symmetry of a young lady's ankles with unparalleled ecstasy. Occasionally others benefited by doing likewise.'

'The beautiful but entirely weird practiser of palmistry believed entirely in the power of syzgy.'

According to OnePoll.com, the word most commonly misspelt (or is that 'misspelled'?) is 'separate'. The eight-letter word came top due to the regular placing of an 'e' where the first 'a' should be. Second is 'definitely' and then 'manoeuvre'; 'embarrass' and 'accommodation' are also high on the list.

"A common mistake," said a spokesperson for the market research company which carried out the survey, "is writing a word the way it sounds, which leaves us muddling up one letter with another and getting it wrong." He continued, "Computer spell-checkers correct words for us but that means we become lazy and never learn the correct spelling."

Well, my computer spell-checker didn't correct one word I had misused. I delighted the headmaster of a grammar school I was intending to visit to undertake a school inspection with my letter.

It should have started 'Dear Headmaster' but it began 'Dear Headamster.' Fortunately, the recipient had a sense of humour and replied, 'Dear Gerbil'.

I am not, of course, alone in sometimes getting a word wrong. The release by Churchill College of the prompt notes of Margaret Thatcher which she used in her speech in 1979 reveals that the former Oxford scholar was not such a brilliant speller. In her jottings of the key words taken from 'The Prayer of St Francis' — discord–harmony/error–truth/doubt–faith — she writes 'dispair' (sic). Fortunately she never attempted the word 'Assisi'.

Another Oxford scholar and future prime minister was little better when it came to spelling. In his biography of Tony Blair, John Rentoul quotes the young Blair's application to be the Labour candidate for Sedgefield. Under 'Previous Experience' the prospective candidate wrote:

'I stood, during the Falklands War, in the Beaconsfield by-election, a Tory seat with a majority [sic] of 23,000.'

Another prime minister, Lord Palmerston, a stickler for correct English, despaired at the poor spelling in the various reports sent to him by his colleagues. In an unexpected test he dictated the following sentence to the eleven cabinet members:

"It is disagreeable to witness the embarrassment of a harassed pedlar gauging the symmetry of a peeled potato."

None of them spelt the words correctly.

There are few things in life which are as reassuring as spotting the mistakes of the great and the good. Writers who are poor spellers find some comfort in the poor spelling of luminaries such as Evelyn Waugh, W B Yeats and F Scott Fitzgerald. And, of course, Shakespeare never spelt his name the same way in any of his six signatures.

Now I guess you are wondering what thirty tricky and trouble-some words make up my 'little test'? Well, here they are. You might like to try them out on family and friends, but be warned: the exercise is likely to cause some argument, so have a dictionary handy.

asinine	liquefy	purify
rarefy	pavilion	vermilion
moccasin	inoculate	impresario
resuscitate	supersede	rococo
mayonnaise	cemetery	titillate
desiccate	sacrilegious	impostor
consensus	minuscule	bureaucracy
canister	predilection	tranquillity
psittacosis	harass	unforeseen
linchpin	misspell	diarrhoea

IT'S THE WAY I SAY IT

Pronunciation

I still recall with great pleasure the occasions when, as a small child, I stood with my father at the kitchen sink as we washed and dried the dishes (which we called the 'pots'). He would launch into a funny poem or a monologue; I thought my father made them up.

> *There's a famous seaside place called Blackpool,*
> *That's noted for its fresh air and fun,*
> *And Mr and Mr Ramsbottom,*
> *Went there with young Albert, their son.*

The following week, after hearing this monologue (which, I discovered later, was called 'The Lion and Albert', made famous by Stanley Holloway), I was listening with the other children to Miss Wilkinson, headmistress of Broom Valley Infant School, telling us in the assembly to sit up smartly and rub the sleep out of our eyes.

"You are a lot of sleepyheads this morning," she told the six year olds sitting crossed-legged before her on the hall floor. Then she asked, "Does anyone know another word for 'sleepy'?" I imagine she was looking for a word like 'tired' but I raised my hand.

"Yes, Gervase?" she asked.

"Somyoolent," I replied, with all the precocious confidence of an infant. This was a word used in the monologue to describe the 'posture' of the sleepy old lion, Wallace.

It was years later, after many recitations of the monologue, that someone pointed out to me that the word was actually pronounced 'somnolent'. I have to admit I still have problems with the word.

It is a fact that many of us have trouble in getting our tongues around bothersome words. In some cases the cause is confusion with a similar-sounding word of quite a different meaning but in others it is ignorance of the word's composition.

I had an education lecturer at college who got in a great tangle trying to pronounce 'pedagogy' (ped-a-go-gee), 'ethnicity' (eth-nis-i-tee), 'phenomenon' (fi-nom-uh-non) and 'philosophical' (fil-uh-sof-i-kuhl).

At an interview for a teaching post a candidate asked what the 'remuneration' (which he pronounced 're-noo-mer-a-shun') would be, and in a recent message from a call-centre a young woman said a representative would be in the area in February (which she pronounced 'Feb-yoo-ary'). I was tempted to correct the mispronunciations — 'ri-myoo-nuh-reyshun' and 'Feb-roo-er-ee' — but resisted. There but for the grace of God ...

Research on pronunciation was recently undertaken by Spinvox (a voicemail-to-text-message system which corrects the inaccurate pronunciation of words). It was discovered that there are a surprising number of commonly used words that we get wrong, words like 'anaesthetist', 'statistics', 'conflagration', 'provocatively', 'anonymous', 'thesaurus', 'regularly' and 'aluminiun.'

Mispronunciation, of course, is no laughing matter, for when we get it wrong it is deeply embarrassing, particularly if some helpful person points it out.

Of course, people dispute as to which is the correct pronunciation on words such as controversy/controversy. Should the emphasis be in the first three letters or the third, fourth and fifth?

My geography master at A-Level insisted on pronouncing the word 'discipline' by stressing the first two letters, and the word 'horizon' with a short 'i'.

In the *Longman Pronunciation Dictionary*, Professor J C Wells lists a selection of commonly mispronounced words, which include:

Anything (anythink)   arthritis (artheritis)
certificate (cerstificate)   dachshund (dash-hound)
deteriorate (deteerorate)   etcetera (ecsetera)
genealogist (geneologist)   grievous (grievious)
aitch (haitch)   integral (intregal)
percolate (perculate)   itinerary (itinary)
meteorologist (meteologist)   recognize (reconize)
relevant (revelant)   secretary (secetary)
supernumerary (supernumary)   temporary (tempory)

What is more, words that may be second nature for English speakers can be doubly difficult for those learning English as a foreign language, as this anonymous poem points out:

Hints on English Pronunciation for Foreigners

I take it you already know
Of tough and bough and cough and dough?
Others may stumble, but not you
On hiccough, thorough, laugh and through?
Well done! And now you wish perhaps
To learn of these familiar traps?

Beware of heard, a dreadful word,
That looks like beard and sounds like bird.

And dead: it's said like bed, not bead,
For goodness' sake, don't call it deed!

Watch out for meat and great and threat,
They rhyme with suite and straight and debt.

A moth is not a moth in mother
Nor both in bother, broth in brother.

And here is not a match for there,
Nor dear and fear for bear and pear.

And then there's does and rose and lose —
Just look them up: and goose and choose.

And cork and front and word and ward
And font and front and word and sword.
And do and go and thwart and cart...

Come, come, I've hardly made a start!
A dreadful language? Man alive,
I'd mastered it when I was five!

The pronunciation of the word 'bath' has always been a source of dispute between North and South. The other day in a department store in Doncaster I overheard a Yorkshireman giving the word a southern touch. It had become a 'barth'.

Later I asked a young man from the South, now long-resident in Yorkshire, what he said for 'bath'. He wasn't sure.

"You see," he explained, "the people I'm living with have got me into the way of calling it a 'wesh-all-ovver'."

A Southern woman became a teacher at a Bradford school. On her first day there she accumulated a quantity of rubbish, so left her classroom in search of the dustbin, and met with another teacher.

"Where's the bin?" she enquired.

"Ah've bin t' toilet, if it's owt to do wi' thee," came the blunt reply.

"I can read all the letters without a problem
— I just can't pronounce the flipping word!"

My friend Alban, who farms near Whitby and is a plain-speaking Yorkshireman with a wry sense of humour, tells the story of when he was at school.

"I'll tell thee what," Alban said, 'I can't get mi 'ead round this stuff abaat speykin' proper. We say 'path', and t' teacher says 'paath', we say 'grass' and she says 'graas', we say 'luck' and she says 'loook', we say 'buck' and she says 'boook'. It's reight confusin'."

"Tha dooan't wants to tek no notice," his brother told him.

"Nay, we've got to practise it for next week. Dust thy know then, dust tha say 'eether' or dust tha say 'ayether'?"

His elder brother thought for a moment before replying.

"Dun't mek no difference 'ow tha says it. Tha can say owther on 'em."

In a similar vein, the pronunciation of 'neither' has ever been a debatable point. Two men were arguing on the correct way to say it; one said 'neether', the other said it was 'nyther'. It took a Yorkshireman to solve their problem: "Noather on yer's reight."

An optician in a Yorkshire Dales market town was testing a farm lad's eyesight. He hung a test card on the wall and asked him to read the top line which ran: S P T Z F K Y L.

The lad screwed up his face and stared at the letters until the optician said impatiently:

"Come, now, surely you can read those big letters."

"Aye," said the lad. "Ah can read 'em all reet, but Ah can't pronounce the word."

A little lad was being taken for a bus ride in the Dales by his mother. The bus crossed a bridge over the River Wharfe.

"Look, mam," he exclaimed, "there's a waterfall."

"Weir, dear," gently reproved his mother.

"Theer," the little lad replied.

"I'M AN OPTOMETRIST; I ALWAYS LOOK ON THE BRIGHT SIDE OF LIFE"

Malapropisms and mishearings

The name malapropism, which comes from the French *mal a propos* (meaning 'not appropriate'), is a term coined from the name of a ludicrous character in Richard Sheridan's comedy *The Rivals*, written in 1775. The word has come to stand for the comical misuse of language.

Mrs Malaprop is an "old weather-beaten she-dragon" who prides herself on the use of the King's English.

"Sure if I reprehend [apprehend] anything in this world," she announces, "it is the use of my oracular [vernacular] tongue and a nice derangement [arrangement] of epitaphs! [epithets]"

In Sheridan's play Mrs Malaprop urges her niece Lydia, who is "as headstrong as an allegory [alligator] on the banks of the Nile", to beware of men for they are "all Bulgarians" (barbarians) and to "illiterate" (obliterate) a certain gentleman from her memory.

Mrs Malaprop also informs her brother that she has interceded (intercepted) a letter to Lydia who "has persisted [desisted] in corresponding with him", and that "my affluence [influence] over my niece is very small".

"Oh!", she exclaims, "it gives me the hydrostatics [hysterics] to such a degree."

Mrs Malaprop was not the first character in literature to misuse words with comic effect. Shakespeare has many characters highly comedic by nature. Dogberry, the self-satisfied watchman in *Much Ado About Nothing*, is comic relief in the play. He is memorable in that he constantly uses malapropisms in his speech:

> "Only get the learned writer to set down our excommunication [examination], and meet me at the jail."

> "One word, sir. Our watch, sir, have indeed comprehended [apprehended] two auspicious [suspicious] persons, and we would have them this morning examined before your worship."

> "Is our whole dissembly [assembly] appeared?"

> "O villain! Thou wilt be condemned into everlasting redemption [damnation] for this."

In *The Expedition of Humphry Clinker*, the last of the picaresque novels of Tobias Smollett, published in 1771, Tabitha, the sister of Matthew Bramble, a Welsh squire, remarks to her maid Winifred:

"I know that hussy, Mary Jones, loves to be rumping [romping] with the men."

Later Winifred remarks that "You who live in the country have no deception [conception] of our doings at Bath."

One of the highlights of our family holiday week in Blackpool when I was a boy was the evening out at the variety show in the theatre on the South Pier. There I saw one of the greatest exponents of the malapropism: the incomparable Hylda Baker.

With her silent stooge, Cynthia, who managed to keep a face as rigid and serious as a death mask throughout the performance, this small woman (four foot eleven inches) in her moth-eaten fox fur, ill-fitting checked jacket, large handbag over the arm and in a misshapen hat, mangled and murdered the language with malapropisms to great comic effect.

Hylda Baker was a direct descendant of Mrs Malaprop, and the precursor of Connie, a character in my Dales series of books.

Hylda had the audience rolling in the aisles with her facial contortions and her misuse of English. She would wriggle her body as if she suffered from chronic worms, crimp her hair, adjust her massive handbag and announce to the audience as she came on stage: "I don't think you've had the pleasure of me".

"I can say this without fear of contraception," she would go on to say. "I went to the doctor and he was stood standing there, his horoscope round his neck. He said I had the body of a woman twice my age. 'You flatterer, you', I said. I nearly had a coronary trombonist and fell prostitute on the floor."

After one show I waited by the stage door for her autograph.

"Have you been stood standing there, have you, you little man?" she asked of the wide-eyed little boy. I nodded. "I bet you've been to the Blackpool illucinations, haven't you?"

However, Hylda Baker's comic misuse of language was not popular with some. It is reputed that when she appeared at the Stephen Joseph Theatre in Scarborough, Noel Coward observed, after the performance he had 'endured', that "I would wring that woman's neck — if I could find it."

Connie, in my Dales books, has a delightfully eccentric command of the English language. She is a mistress of the malapropism and a skilled practitioner of the non sequitur. For Connie, English is not a dull and dreary business; it is something to twist and play with, distort, invent and reinterpret.

There was the occasion when she reported that her daughter had been unsuccessful at the interview for a job.

"Of course," Connie confided, "she's far too self-defecating."

I did remark mischievously that this would certainly go against her.

When she mislaid her precious stepladders, Connie announced that she would "leave no rolling stone upturned" until she found them, and vowed "to take the bull between the horns" and tackle the suspected culprit.

On another occasion, when some teachers complained that they couldn't hear one of the speakers who was delivering a lecture in the main hall, she agreed that the "agnostics" were not too good in that particular room.

Once she grumbled that one of the inspectors had made a complaint to her boss about the state of the toilets in the teachers' centre.

"I don't know who it is who has made these allegations," she says angrily, "but if I find out who the alligator is, I shall give him a piece of my mind."

I am quick to note down a malapropism if I hear one. On a cruise ship I overheard the contretemps of a man and his wife as they stood leaning on the rail and looking out over the harbour:

She: You've done nothing but moan since you got on the boat.

He: It's a ship.

She: I don't care what it is, you've moaned and groaned since we walked up the plank.

He: I've got a right to moan. We come on the world tour and we're stuck here looking at Southampton gasworks.

She: Shurrup. Worse things can happen at sea.

He: That's just it. We're not at sea, are we?

She: You want to think yourself lucky. You'd soon complain if you were swept out to sea on a satsuma.

Once I was in a café, and at the next table was a mum and her young children. The youngsters were becoming increasingly fractious. The woman decided she had to take action to quieten her brood. She mustered a glare of annoyance and warned them:

"If you don't behave, I'll run away and join the British Legion."

My friend Joan, who owns a shop in Skipton, North Yorkshire, has collected these examples from colleagues and customers:

> She took me to a pub for a meal — sausage and mash, and lovely homemade lanzarote. (lasagna)
> My granddaughter takes electrocution lessons.
> Her aunt is going to a wedding so she went to the hat shop to buy a fornicater. (fascinator)
> My sister went to hospital to have a monogram.
> She has had a skylark fitted in the loft.
> Delighted I can ring my daughter in lasagna [Lanzarote] now she has had a land mine fitted.
> A nice commode to go under her suit jacket. (camisole)
> She banks with the Alien and Leicester.
> I enjoyed the Paralytic Games.
> My pregnant daughter had painful contraptions.
> The doctor had left his testicles on the table. (spectacles)
> I've wiped the compensation off the windows.
> Sorry to hear about her belligerent tumour.
> She recommended artificial insinuation.
> She was so thin and emancipated.

Here are some more memorable malapropisms:

> Her house was state of the ark.
> Let's talk about a very tattoo subject.
> She has in this interior desecrator.
> The place was full of lymphomanicas.
> Patience is a virgin.
> She gave him artificial reincarnation.
> He's over ninety but in full possession of all his facilities.
> She's got a congenial hip disease.
> In her elastic stockings, next to her very close veins.
> What you say is totally irreverent.
> He's a wolf in cheap clothing.

She said honesty was the best politics.

It's just another faucet of his personality.

Theirs is a purely plutonic relationship.

She's fluid in French you know.

I can't stand the taste of that evacuated milk.

She's got very good testimonicals.

It compromises the total.

They divorced because they were always at locker heads.

She tells a lovely antidote.

She's receiving private intuition.

He's got a lot of prefixes after his name.

Good to get my feet back on terra cotta.

He had to go to the solicitor to sign a Happy David.

It serves ornamental food.

The bedroom has a built in sanitary unit.

The flu outbreak has reached pandemonium stage.

He exhumed confidence.

It's merely a pigment of his imagination.

I can't stand heights because I suffer from virago.

He's got channel vision.

I might just fade into Bolivian, know what I mean?

It's beyond my apprehension.

There's no stigmata attached to being red-headed.

It was a heart-rendering story, most pungent at the end.

She fired a shot across his bowels.

Be more pacific.

I hear the ocean is infatuated with sharks.

Work is my only solstice.

Do you take this man to be your awful wedded husband?

She's always casting dispersions.

She gets her tablets from the hospital suppository.

It's a mute point.

The old soldier was shuffling from shell shock.

We talk about one thing, then she goes off on a tandem.

She had the wart removed by local euthanasia.

If you suffer from allegories please make this known to
the catering staff.

All this gerrymeandering makes me angry.

I was given an old tomato: leave or get thrown out.

She had her toenails done — one of these pedigrees.

He was given a standing ovulation.

I was ignored and made to feel like a social piranha.

They had to use a needle to seduce him.

He's in gainful underemployment.

He used polyurinated varnish in the floor.

It was all in this sadistical report.

He was taken to hospital with damage to his cartridge.

It's all par for the corpse.

We need to flush out all the details.

This job should be easy — it's not rocket salad.

He's suffering from manic repression.

All this politically corrupt language.

She's asphyxiated with the man.

Sorry for my incontinence.

She's seeing a psychopath for her bad back.

They used artificial dissemination.

The front tyre had flatulence.

She's as ignorant as they come — a real Palestinian.

She's had her utopian tubes tied.

We had these Geneva Witnesses knocking at the door.

I think you've completely misconceived what I said.

Just a few bruises and minor contortions.

Hair up in a buffoon style.

He's very ego-testicle.

They served soup out of a big silver latrine.

He had this Dober Pincherman dog.

It will suffice for all intensive purposes.

She's Mary in the naivety play at school.

And just what are you incinerating?

It's a purely epidemic question.

The bomb alert meant the city was evaporated.

In the Morecambe and Wise TV series, Ernie explains the plot of "a play wot I wrote" called The Handyman and M'Lady (a parody of *Lady Chatterley's Lover*):

"It's about a man who has an accident with a combine harvester, which unfortunately makes him impudent."

Politicians are not above getting their words mixed up.

The then US vice-president Dan Quayle, famous for correcting a child's correct spelling of 'potato', stressed "the importance of bondage between a mother and children".

Former president George W Bush once announced that "We can't let terriers [terrorists] and rogue nations hold this nation hostile or hold our allies hostile." On another occasion he said he recognised "the fallacy [fallibility] of humans".

"Do we use the term intervention, do we use war, do we use squirmishes?" asked vice-president hopeful, Sara Palin, talking about the action in Libya.

Our own politicians, too, sometimes come a cropper. Tobias Elwood, MP for Bournemouth, complimented the Speaker in the House of Commons.

"You are an anecdote of verbal diarrhoea," he said.

As a school inspector, I was once in an infants class which had been learning all about sums and the different words for them.

"What is the total?" the teacher asked.

"The total," replied one little boy, "is what you get when you add up all the numbers."

"And what is the remainder?" the teacher then asked.

"The remainder, miss, is the animal what pulls Santa's sleigh."

"Just what are you incinerating? You completely misconceive
what I said, have asked a purely epidemic question that is
completely beyond my apprehension, and moreover what you
say is totally irreverent, so please be more pacific."

On her way home on the school bus, a young lass was singing to herself. The conductor, who was not familiar with the words, asked her what she was singing. The little lass replied:

"Them words is my own composure."

And there but for the grace of God go we all. One particular Christmas I wanted to give my wife Christine, who is a keen gardener, a propagator. At Wentworth Garden Centre I asked the assistant if she sold 'incubators'.

"We don't grow babies," she told me.

Related to the malapropism is the 'mondegreen'. This is a mishearing or misinterpretation of a phrase. American writer Sylvia Wright coined the term in her essay 'The Death of Lady Mondegreen', published in 1954. She wrote of how, when growing up, she had listened to a ballad called 'The Bonny Earl O'Moray' and misheard one of the lines:

"When I was a child, my mother used to read aloud to me from *Percy's Reliques*, and one of my favorite poems began, as I remember:

> *Ye Highlands and ye Lowlands,*
> *Oh, where hae ye been?*
> *They hae slain the Earl O' Moray,*
> *And Lady Mondegreen.*"

The actual last line was 'And laid him on the green'. Sylvia coined a new term for this kind of mishearing, and observed:

"The point about what I shall hereafter call mondegreens, since no one else has thought up a word for them, is that they are better than the original."

I once received a letter from a mother who had taken her young daughter to hear me speak. I mentioned my Uncle Ted as a Dunkirk veteran. Later the child, when asked by her grandmother could she remember anything I had said, said:

"His Uncle Ted was a drunken vegetarian."

I was told the story of the member of parliament who was being quizzed about his excessive expenses.

In his defence he said, "I've got the chits."

"I bet you have," mumbled the auditor.

The mondegreen is most commonly applied to a line in a poem or in the lyric in a song. Here are few of my favourites:

> 'Bad Moon Rising' by Creedence Clearwater Revival:
> 'There's a bathroom on the right.'
> ('There's a bad moon on the rise.')

> 'Lucy in the Sky with Diamonds' by the Beatles:
> 'Lucy in Disguise with Diamonds.'

> 'Lucy in the Sky with Diamonds':
> 'The girl with colitis goes by.'
> ('The girl with kaleidoscope eyes.')

> 'The Girl from Ipanema' by Astrud Gilberto:
> 'The girl with emphysema goes walking.'

> 'What a Wonderful World' by Louis Armstrong:
> 'The bright blessed day and the dog said goodnight.'
> ('The bright blessed day, the dark sacred night.')

> 'Natural Woman' by Carol King:
> 'You're the cheese to my pizza mine.'
> ('You're the key to my piece of mind.')

> 'You Can't Hurry Love' by the Supremes:
> 'Cranberry love, no you just have to wait.'

I remember that, when a boy, I would deliberately sing the alternative to the words in the carol 'While shepherds watched their flocks by night' as 'While shepherds washed their socks by night.' Sometimes, however, children genuinely mishear the words of carols and hymns, and teachers report some very amusing alternatives such as:

> "Get dressed ye married gentlemen,
> Let nothing through this May."

> "Good King Wences' car backed out,
> On the feet of heathens."

Here are a few examples of mondegreens from children reputedly overheard as they said their prayers:

> From Psalm 23:
> "Surely Good Mrs Murphy shall follow me all the days of my life."

> From 'The Lord's Prayer':
> "Our Father who art in heaven, Harold be thy name."

> From 'The Lord's Prayer':
> "And lead us not into temptation but deliver us our email."

> From 'The Lord's Prayer':
> "Our Father who shops in Hebbon."

> From 'The Hail Mary':
> "Hail Mary, full of grace, the Lord is with thee.
> Blessed art thou, a monk swimming."

"In love, as in life, one misheard word can be tremendously important ... If you tell someone you love them, for instance, you must be absolutely certain that they have replied, 'I love you back' and not 'I love your back' before you continue the conversation."

Lemony Snicket, *Horseradish: the Bitter Truths You Can't Avoid*

I well recall the first school governing body I addressed as an OFSTED inspector. The serious-faced group sat before me, all eyes trained in my direction. The chair of governors, a florid-faced man with huge ginger eyebrows which curved into question marks, eyed me suspiciously with pale watery eyes.

"We're 'ere for the report from the school inspector," he announced. "This is Mr Flynn from OFFSET."

"Off what?" enquired a plain-faced little woman with a pursed mouth and small black darting eyes.

"No, no, that's the water, Doris. Mr Flynn's from OFFSET."

"OFSTED," I corrected him, "and it's Mr Phinn."

"OFSTED?" he repeated, "is that what it is?"

"OFFSET is, as I remember, a machine which prints paper," I said, smiling.

"I think I was right fust time with OFSETT, Mr Flynn," announced the chairman of governors. "Talk about churning out paper. I reckon when you do your inspections a forest falls."

At a governors' meeting in a primary school, one rather precious woman bemoaned the use by the children "of these dreadful expressions".

"Why, coming across the playground before the meeting," she told her colleagues, "I heard a child call another one a 'cakehole'."

I felt it prudent not to put her right on this one.

In the primary school assembly one Christmas, the children had been singing seasonal songs and carols, including Rudolf the Red Nosed Reindeer. Afterwards in class, the teacher asked the children who was their favourite reindeer: Rudolf, Dancer ...?

"Olive," called out one little girl.

The teacher thought for a moment.

"But I didn't know there was a reindeer called Olive."

"Oh yes, miss. It's in the song: 'Olive the other reindeer, used to laugh and call him names'."

The 'Four Candles' sketch (originally titled 'The Hardware Shop' or 'Annie Finkhouse)' is a sketch from the BBC comedy series

The Two Ronnies. It contains a wonderfully inventive set of mondegreens, and illustrates Ronnie Barker's fascination with and command of the English language.

The shopkeeper in a hardware shop becomes increasingly frustrated by a customer because he misunderstands the various requests. The customer asks for what sounds like 'four candles' and is handed the said products, only to be told it was 'fork 'andles', he wanted — handles for forks.

When the shopkeeper is asked for 'peas', thinking the customer is wanting the letter 'P' for the garden gate, he gets down a box of letters only to be informed it is "peas, tins of peas" that are wanted. And so the confusion with words continues.

There was a Yorkshire farmer who, having won the Lottery, visited an upmarket shop which boasted it could create life-sized models of anything in solid gold. Having the 'brass', the farmer thought he would have Shep, his faithful collie, immortalised.

"Eighteen carats?" asked the shop assistant.

"Nay, lad," replied the farmer. "I wants 'im chewing on a bone."

The teacher in the Dales school was reading from the Scriptures.

"Blessed are they that mourn…" and then interjected: "What is to mourn, Christopher?"

Replied the little lad brightly: "Wednesday."

In Leeds magistrates' court, a loquacious witness was told by the presiding magistrate to be a little more terse in his evidence.

"I suppose you know what terse means?" asked the magistrate.

"Course I do — it's t' first coach at a funeral."

In the 1930s an urban district council in South Yorkshire had completed its first council housing estate, and the housing committee sat in solemn conclave, trying to find a name for it.

"That's easy," said one of the members. "Ah reckon that we owt ter cal 'em T' Cloisters."

"Cloisters?" exclaimed the others, mystified.

"Aye, because they're clois ter t' shops, they're clois ter t' pub, they're clois ter t' cinema, they're clois ter t' church, they're clois ter t' cemetry. They're clois ter ivverything."

Old Enoch lived in a Dales village with his ailing wife. He was usually to be found sitting near the cottage door making odds and ends out of timber he found round about the village.

One day, when the doctor called, Enoch was sitting outside hammering nails into some pieces of wood.

"How is your wife today?" asked the doctor.

"Oh pretty bad, sir, pretty bad."

"Is that her coughing?"

"Oh no," said Enoch, "this is a chicken coop."

Two youngsters were sitting in the kitchen playing 'I Spy'.

Billy (a true Yorkshireman) said 'T'; and Tommy (from Essex), after guessing 'table', 'teaspoon', 'tea towel' and so on, gave up.

Triumphantly, Billy said:

"T' oven door."

The junior school class, in a village at the foot of the Pennines, was studying spelling. The teacher was explaining how the letter Q is always followed by the letter U. Examples were flowing freely, and the word 'quoit' was given.

"Anyone not know what a quoit is?" asked the teacher.

The class looked mystified.

"Michael," said the teacher, "go and fetch me a quoit."

Off went Michael, proud and pleased to be chosen, and returned triumphantly — with his overcoat.

Farmer George was asked how his son, who was at agricultural college, was coming along with his studies.

"Well, tha knows," replied Farmer George, "he still ploughs t' same way, but he talks different. He allus used to say 'Whoa, Ned'

when he gat to th' end o' t' furrow, and then it was 'Gee up, lad'.
Now he's that posh he says, 'Halt, Edward; pivot and proceed.'
T' horse can't understand him. So I'm telling you, it's no good
sending anybody away to learn farming unless tha sends t' horse
an' all."

Some tongue-in-cheek suggestions for an 'alternative' Yorkshire
dictionary:
    retail - proper Yorkshire bitter
    towel - what a night-hunting bird is known as in Yorkshire
    twirled - everywhere else, as seen from Yorkshire

Two small boys stood looking up at the statue of Sir Titus Salt in
Manningham Park, Bradford. One of them read out the title
inscribed underneath: "Sir Titus Salt, Bart."
    Turning to the other one he said: "What does 'Bart' mean?"
    The other one looked up at the statue again and replied:
    "Why, baht 'at, of course."

"When I was little we had a dog called Grieg, after t' composer."
    "That's odd. Did it like classical music or summat?"
    "No, it used to pee agin t' suite."

NEVER BOLT THE DOOR WITH A BOILED CARROT

Proverbs

"Proverbs are short sentences drawn from long experiences." (Cervantes, 1547-1616)

"Proverbs receive their chief value from the stamp and esteem of ages through which they have passed." (Sir William Temple, 1622-99)

Years ago, over the summer holidays I used to teach foreign students in an independent school in Sussex. The boys, most of whom could speak some English, all came to this country for the six-week intensive course to improve their command of the language. One German student called Klaus was disappointed to find that none of the teachers used what he called 'zer proberb'.

"In Germany," he told me, "Herr Kobberger teaches us that in England all the people use proberbs."

I did point out to him that, sadly, few people in England now use proverbs in their everyday spoken language, which was a shame, for these short pithy aphorisms, which have a long history, add immeasurably to the richness of the language.

It is a commonly held view that the proverb is a hackneyed expression used by people who are unable to express their thoughts with clarity or originality. This is not the case, for the

proverb encapsulates a complex thought and offers, in a few short words, sensible advice.

"Acquaint thyself with proverbs," it says in Ecclesiasticus, "for of them thou shalt learn instruction."

There is a countless number of proverbs. Here are a few of my favourites:

> There is a remedy for everything but death.
>
> When the wind fails, take to the oars.
>
> Have a care of a silent dog and still water.
>
> Handsome is as handsome does.
>
> You cannot put a saddle on an ox.
>
> It is easy to be generous with other people's property.
>
> It's a wise child that knows its own father.
>
> Many kiss the child for the mother's sake.
>
> Thin ice and thick ice look the same from a distance.
>
> A bald man needs no comb.
>
> Admiration is the offspring of ignorance.
>
> Envy has no holidays.
>
> He who goes to law holds a wolf by the ears.
>
> A blow with a word strikes deeper than a blow with a sword.
>
> One dog can't fight.
>
> In the choicest vase are found the ugliest cracks.
>
> Never let your mother comb your hair after an argument.

My parents, both lovers of language, would chuckle after the visit of an elderly neighbour, for she frequently mixed up the proverbs to great comic effect.

"We'll burn that bridge when we come to it," she would say; and "She needs to take the bull by the tail".

Here are a few other mixed-up proverbs:

> A leopard cannot change its stripes.
>
> Strike when the iron is in the fire.
>
> Every colour under the rainbow.
>
> Never kick a gift horse in the mouth.
>
> It's an open and dry case.
>
> You can kiss that down the drain.
>
> Every silver lining has a rain cloud behind it.

My Grannie Mullarkey had a wonderful turn of phrase, a quality often possessed by the Irish. Here are few of her adages:

> She's so good she bites the altar rails.
>
> He's not long for the world, for he has the smell of clay on him.
>
> She had a smile like last month's rhubarb.
>
> He has eyes like a couple of fried eggs.
>
> He's as much use as a grave robber in a crematorium.
>
> He's so quiet he comes into the room like a drop of soot.
>
> She has a mouth like a torn pocket.
>
> She has a tongue that would clip tin.
>
> If he died with a face like that, nobody would wash the corpse.
>
> It runs in the family like Mrs O'Hara's nose.
>
> He's so fond of work, he'd lie down beside it.
>
> If he was thrown after you, you wouldn't turn round to see what the clatter was.

As a child, the meaning of one of my grandmother's favourite proverbs was beyond me. I am still not quite sure what it means:

> 'Never bolt the door with a boiled carrot.'

THE LORD IS A SHOVING LEOPARD

Spoonerisms

The spoonerism is a form of metathesis (the transformation of sounds or letters in a word) so as to form some ridiculous combination. Most of us have heard a small child refer to a 'flutterby' (butterfly).

The term spoonerism is named after Rev William Spooner (1844-1930), warden of New College, Oxford, a fast-talking and noted academic. Some of the best examples attributed to him are:

> "Kinkering kongs their titles take."
> (Conquering kings their titles take)

> "I have in my bosom a half-warmed fish."
> (half-formed wish)

> "The defeat was a blushing crow."

> Proposing a toast to Queen Victoria:
> "Three cheers for our queer old dean!"

> "Well-boiled icicle" (well-oiled bicycle)

> When performing a wedding ceremony:
> "It is kisstomary to cuss the bride."

> "The enemy fled quickly from the ears and sparrows."

Wishing to see to the college dean, he asked his secretary:
"Is the bean dizzy?"

On dropping his hat:
"Will no one pat my hiccup?"

"Those girls are sin twisters."

On entering church for Sunday service:
"Good grief, someone is occupewing my pie."

"There is no peace in a home where a dinner swells."

"The Lord is a shoving leopard."

During the First World War, he told his students:
"When the boys come back from France, we'll have the hags flung out."

"Let me sew you to your sheet."

"She joins this club over my bed doddy."

"Let us sing the old revival hymn 'Shall We Rather At the Giver?'."

Greeting a group of farmers: "I see before me tons of soil." (sons of toil)

"You have hissed my mystery lectures and were caught fighting a liar in the quad. Having tasted the whole worm, you will leave by the next town drain."

Spoonerisms are usually the result of the speaker's tiredness or speed of talking when the tongue cannot keep pace with the speaker's thoughts. Some of my favourites are:

The Queen was greeted with a twenty-one son galoot.

The navy had many cattle ships and bruisers.

"The Lord is a shoving leopard…"

She has moved into a new flock of bats.

He fought the blaze with an ex-tyre finguisher.

Everything happened in one swell foop.

Now you are just pit nicking.

If you're dirty, go and shake a tower.

Stop nicking your pose!

Stanley Gibbons was a famous damp stealer.

You have very mad banners.

The car had a bat flattery.

The President of the United States, Hubert Heever.

It's all a lack of pies.

Look outside, it's roaring with pain.

Mother Teresa's mission was sealing the hick.

The Devil is a bowel feast.

Come and wook out of the lindow.

The British Broadcorping Castration.

The doctor injected him with a hypodemic nurdle.

She was fundraising to raise money to wave the sails.

If you've got a cold, know your blows.

Now this is the pun fart.

When I banged my arm I hit my bunny phone.

The bride heard the sound of bedding wells.

Bugs Bunny is a cartoon runny babbit.

The cottage had lots of nosey little cooks and crannies.

The chocolate cake was decorated with nasal huts.

Einstein was fascinated by the lead of spite.

Sometimes the term is applied to the switch of complete words, as in:

'Children should be heard and not seen'.

This kind of spoonerism lends itself to deliberate word play, as when Oscar Wilde observed that

"Work is the curse of the drinking classes."

The Archbishop of Canterbury, Dr Cosmo Lang, was invited to a luncheon hosted by Mervyn Hayt, the Bishop of Coventry. One of the guests was a nervous young curate who, in his confusion, suggested to the distinguished cleric:

"Have another piece of grace, your cake."

Like many parents, when my children were small, I noted down their little gems of language which included some memorable Spoonerisms:

Dominic:	May I have some more keys and parrots please?
Elizabeth:	It's teepy slime
	The bater wottle is leaking
Richard :	I've known my blows
Matthew:	I've burt my hunny phone
	May I have some cop porn please?

A class of eleven-year-olds I once taught found my instruction highly amusing when I said:

"Would all the goys and birls line up please?"

SHEDDING A TEAR FOR NELSON

Euphemisms

As I child growing up in Rotherham in the 1950s I was frequently baffled by the terms adults used. They made no sense. In the queue in the tripe shop, I would overhear the conversation of the proprietor (a large woman with a bay window of a bust which she would rest on the counter) and her customers. Suddenly she would lower her voice and, looking in my direction, remark that "Little rabbits have big ears", before vouchsafing some snippet of gossip.

"Of course, she's no better than she should be," she would say of the girl who worked in the chip shop. "Puts it about a bit, from what I hear. Course, her sister was eating for two before she was sixteen — if you follow my drift."

Here was the precursor of Les Dawson's Ada. The tripe shop lady would mouth something which made no sense to me at all.

"She's had it all taken away," she said of her neighbour, "and her husband's had an operation in the downstairs department."

When I went for a haircut with my father, I was intrigued when, with lowered voice, the barber asked him:

"Anything for the weekend?"

When I questioned my father what the barber meant, I was told to wait until I was older. So, at an early age, I was introduced to the euphemism.

As a young lad growing up in rural Yorkshire in the 1950s, Terry Wilson also went to a traditional men's barber, as he relates in his book *A Boy's Own Dale*:

"I always thought of him as a responsible kind of man because he had this clock with a sign on it saying 'Surgical Rubberware' — ready for any unexpected accident, I supposed.

"He was also very thoughtful. As his customers paid up and were about to leave, he always asked if they'd like anything for the weekend. If they nodded, he'd reach under the counter, put a small packet in a brown bag and pass it over.

"I tried it once after my short back and sides. I asked him if I could have something for the weekend. He looked at my short pants, reached down under the counter and passed me a small brown bag. It explained why he was always so discreet when I saw what was inside. I could understand grown men being too embarrassed to ask for sherbet lollies."

H W Fowler's definition is that a euphemism is "The use of a mild or vague or periphrastic expression as a substitute for blunt precision or disagreeable use" (*Modern English Usage*, 1957).

We use euphemisms when dealing with a sensitive subject.

"It is the language of evasion, hypocrisy, prudery and deceit," argues R W Holder in *How Not to Say What You Mean*.

Once, visiting a convent high school, I enquired of the headmistress, a small, bright-eyed nun, if I might "wash my hands". She directed me to a room with just a row of hooks and a small washbasin. I returned to her study. "Actually, sister, I was wanting the toilet."

"Why didn't you say you needed the lavatory, Mr Phinn?" she said with a wry smile. I am certain she knew what I meant in the first place but was just being mischievous.

Euphemisms tend to cluster around four principal taboo subjects: bodily functions, death, sex and disease.

There must be hundreds of euphemistic descriptions for the toilet: 'the little boy's room', the place where one 'spends a penny', 'powders one's nose', 'washes one's hands,' 'checks on the scones', 'performs the usual offices', 'sees a man about a dog', 'answers the call of Nature', 'pays a visit to the House of Commons'.

It's called the 'convenience', 'powder room', 'comfort station', 'rest room', 'cloakroom', 'smallest room', 'bathroom', 'indoor facility', 'hoo-hah', 'loo' and 'necessary' amongst many other things.

When I was in America I heard it frequently referred to as 'the John' and the 'WC' and once interestingly as 'the honey bucket.'

I am reliably informed that when members of the royal family want 'to pay a visit', they inform their hosts that they 'wish to retire'.

Mark, my books editor at Dalesman, tells me that in Spain a customary phrase translates into English as 'I am going to change the canary's water'.

At a naval dinner which I attended, the officer next to me 'excused himself' with the words "I'm going to shed a tear for Nelson".

On another occasion the very word itself became a euphemism when a lady informed me she was "going to the euphemism".

A G Marsden of Wakefield offered this addition to my growing collection of euphemistic terms for toilets:

"I was in Kenya in the 1950s, and although the towns had modern sewerage systems, up country things could be a bit more primitive. After dark it was customary for the men to go outside 'to look at Africa'."

The most interesting toiletary euphemism was told to me by Nigel Reece, who devised and chairs the Radio Four programme *Quote-Unquote*. We were speaking at the Yorkshire Post Literary Lunch and he amused the audience with the story of the rather precious

"I'm desperate to shed a tear for Nelson."

woman, who, when she wished to visit the said place, would tell her companions that she was "going to turn the vicar's bike around".

Sometimes the use of the euphemism is just plain silly. There is the Bible story (1 Samuel, Chapter 24) in which Saul and his army are pursuing David. David and his men are hiding in the far end of a cave when Saul enters "to relieve himself". In most Bible translations such as the English Revised Version this is the phrase used. However, in the King James' Bible, Saul is described as "covering his feet"; and in the Douay-Rheims version "Saul went to ease himself". In other versions the phrases "do his necessaries" and "perform an act of necessity" are used. One American version takes the euphemism a stage further, stating that Saul "went into the cave to use the bathroom".

The English language contains numerous euphemisms related to dying, death, burial, and the people and places which deal with death.

People don't die, they 'fade away' because 'the end is near'. Loved ones have 'passed away' or 'gone to a better place', 'freed from the trials of life' and 'ready to face their Maker'. They are 'released from earthy care' and 'promoted to glory', and having 'shuffled off this mortal coil' now 'dwell in the land of all forgetfulness' and 'sleep in the arms of Jesus'.

Deceased is a euphemism for 'dead', and a dead person may be referred to as 'late' as in 'the late John Smith'.

Sometimes the 'deceased' or the 'departed' is said to have 'gone to a better place'.

The corpse was once referred to as 'the shroud' or 'house (or tenement) of clay', and funeral directors (formerly described as 'undertakers') often use terms such as 'the loved one' or 'the dearly departed'.

In America, some have given up the euphemism 'mortician' in

favour of 'grief therapist', and hold 'arrangement conferences' with relatives. Among themselves, mortuary technicians often refer to the corpse as 'the client'.

There are many dysphemisms related to death. These are the very opposite of euphemisms — blunt, disrespectful and sometimes downright offensive expressions often used to make something sound worse than it is: 'kicked the bucket', 'wears the wooden overcoat', 'bit the big one', 'bought the farm', 'croaked', 'gave up the ghost', 'gone south', 'assumed room temperature'. When buried, he is 'pushing up daisies' or 'taking a dirt nap'. There are hundreds of such expressions in use.

There are many derogatory terms to describe someone who is not very bright:
> One sausage short of a mixed grill.
> One sandwich short of a picnic.
> Nutty as a fruitcake.
> The buses don't go to where he lives.
> The lift doesn't go to the top floor.
> The light is on but nobody's at home.
> The hamster's dead but the wheel is still turning.
> Not the brightest button in the box.
> One word short of a sentence.

A form of euphemism is doublespeak, which is the deliberate use by governments, military or corporate institutions.

A simple example would be the use of the word 'casualties' instead of deaths or 'taking friendly fire' as a euphemism for being attacked by your own troops.

'Big Stick Diplomacy' is really another way of saying a policy backed up by the threat of military action.

There are a few euphemisms for killing which are respectful or playful; they are rather clinical and detached.

The present 'conflict' in Afghanistan has spawned a whole raft of euphemisms for killing, including: 'armed intervention', 'pacification', 'collateral damage', 'strike', 'encounter', 'neutralise', 'engage', 'contact' and 'termination'.

'Anti-personnel devices' are designed to kill or maim, 'area denial munitions' are landmines, 'pre-dawn vertical insertion' is invasion by helicopter, and bombs which kill civilians are, according to the Pentagon, 'incontinent ordnance'.

'Debriefing' is interrogation and 'enhanced debriefing' is torture.

Someone who is shellshocked has an 'acute environmental reaction' or suffers from 'post-traumatic stress disorder', 'operational exhaustion', or 'battle fatigue'.

Some of this may simply be the use of precise technical terminology in the place of popular usage, the advantage of which is that it lacks any emotional undertones.

Some further examples of euphemisms:

> Motion discomfort receptacle *or* air-sickness container (sick bag)

> Sanitary landfill (rubbish dump)

> Black-coated little workers (prunes with laxative qualities)

> The English Disease (syphilis)

> Bathroom tissue (toilet paper).
> (I once heard a boy returning to the classroom, having been allowed by his teacher to 'pay a visit', announce that there was no 'ammunition' available.)

> Aztec Two-Step *or* Montezuma's Revenge (diarrhoea)

> Laying off, downsizing, adjusting the headcount, restructuring, staff realigning (the firing of employees)

Economical with the truth (lying)

Aesthetic procedure *or* facial enhancement (plastic surgery)

Frank exchange of views (argument)

customer service representative (shop assistant)

ambient replenishment operative (shelf-stacker)

An interesting example of euphemistic usage is when one wishes to point out to someone in company something which might cause that person embarrassment if told in a straightforward way, such as an unzipped fly on a man's trousers.

When I was a boy, the expression to draw someone's attention to this potentially embarrassing situation was 'you're flying low' or 'you need to adjust your dress'. Now we have 'there's a window in your laptop', 'the sailor is trying to take a little shore leave', 'your garage door is open', 'the lion's cage is open' and 'you've got a security breach' — and I guess there are many more.

I was once reproached by a teacher following a talk I had given for using the word 'brainstorm' to describe the classroom practice of getting children to share their ideas.

"We don't use that word any more," I was told. "We use the terms 'thought-shower' or 'cloudburst'."

Now we enter the choppy waters of political correctness...

The philosophy of political correctness emerged in the 1990s in the United States, and promoted the avoidance of terminology which might cause offence or denigrate groups regarded as disadvantaged in some way by race, gender, disability, class or religion. Those in the forefront of this new way of thinking recommended alternatives to certain expressions.

In some cases this substitution of terms traditionally used was long overdue, for example 'Downs Syndrome' for 'Mongol' and 'cerebral palsy' for 'spastic'. Children who were once described as 'backward' and 'retarded' became 'those with special educational needs'.

Being in the 'twilight years' myself, I prefer to be called a 'senior citizen' rather than 'an old-aged pensioner'.

I do think, however, political correctness is sometimes taken to extremes:

Vertically challenged for short.

Replacement workers for strikebreakers.

Economically disadvantaged for poor.

Economically inactive for unemployed.

Hormonally challenged for difficult teenager.

Such revisionism extends to the rewriting of certain books. It is interesting that in the reprints of the wonderful *Thomas the Tank Engine*, the children's picture books by Rev W Awdry and first published in 1946, the character of the Fat Controller has been replaced. In one version of an American Bible published in 1994, not only most gender-specific words have been substituted, but the phrase 'God's right hand' has been replaced with 'God's hand' for fear of offending the left-handed.

At a recent medical check-up at the Well Person's Clinic I was informed by the nurse that I was 'clinically obese'. Jokingly I retorted that she was guilty of weightism — discrimination on the grounds of excessive weight. She smiled. Perhaps her bluntness might have the effect of getting me to lose weight, hence she did not waste her time by using one of the many euphemisms for 'fat': 'generously-proportioned', 'big-boned', 'large-framed', 'plump', 'chubby', 'stout', 'stocky', 'well-built' or 'portly'.

Those interested in learning about what we can and cannot say should consult *The Official Politically Correct Dictionary and Handbook* by Henry Beard and Christopher Cerf.

According to Nigel Rees in his *Politically Correct Phrasebook* (1993), the following '-isms' are politically incorrect:

> Alphabetism: discrimination according to the alphabetical position of a person's name.

> Heightism: discrimination against tall women or short men.

> Sightism: discrimination against the blind.

> Uglyism: discrimination on the grounds of unfavourable appearance.

> Smellism: discrimination on the grounds of body odour.

> Handism: discrimination against the left-handed.
> Smokeism: discrimination against smokers.

In *All Gong and no Dinner*, an excellent collection of catchphrases, household sayings and proverbial pearls of wisdom, Nigel Rees refers to the expression 'Johnson's at the door', a euphemism to indicate that someone has a drip on the end of his or her nose.

Nigel recounts the story of how the lady of the manor, plagued with a cold, asked her butler to inform her should he notice a dewdrop. Rather than tell her directly in front of the guests, they decided that he should use the words 'Johnson's at the door' to indicate her runny nose.

At dinner the butler noticed the dewdrop on the end of her ladyship's nose and, as agreed, announced that 'Johnson's at the door'. The lady of the manor had quite forgotten the coded message they had agreed upon.

"I don't know a Johnson," she replied.

The butler tapped his nose. "Johnson is at the door," he repeated.

"Who is this Johnson?" asked his mistress.

"It doesn't matter, your ladyship," the butler told her. "Johnson's in the soup."

RIP OFF YOUR GONADS BEFORE ITALIAN VIRGINS

Mnemonics

Mnemonics (from the Greek *mnemon* meaning 'mindful') are words which assist our memory, and they certainly helped me through many an examination.

Most of us recall how we learnt the colours of the rainbow and could chant them off in the correct order:

'Richard Of York Gave Battle In Vain.'

I have come across another version, 'Round Old York Great Buildings I View', and did hear of the science master who taught the somewhat risqué alternative of 'Rip Off Your Gonads Before Italian Virgins', but this mnemonic is not something I would recommend teaching children.

I learnt the order of the planets with a useful mnemonic:

'My Very Easy Method Just Speeds Up Naming Planets: Mercury, Venus, Earth, Mars, Jupiter, Saturn, Uranus, Neptune and Pluto.'

In one school I visited, the teacher taught the children mnemonics to help them remember how to spell difficult words:

because: Big Elephants Can Always Understand Small Elephants
weird: When Ever I Run, Disaster!
rhythm: Rejoice Heartily, Your Teacher Has Measles
Embarrass: Every Mother's Boy Acts Rather Rudely After Some Sausages

"So, who has thought of a mnemonic for the remembering colours of the rainbow? Yes, you Jenkins. What's that – 'Rip Off Your Gonads Before Italian Virgins'?!?"

When a teacher I found that many parents had trouble with the word 'diarrhoea' and avoided its use in their notes reporting a child's illness, preferring to use phrases like 'upset tummy'. Thoses who did have a go at it often spelt it incorrectly:

> Dear Sir,
> Simon is off with dire rear which is all down our street.
> Dear Sir,
> Susan is away from school with ~~diea diahrr~~ the runs.

In one particular school, children were asked to devise their own mnemonics to help them remember the correct spellings of words frequently misspelled. One word was 'diarrhoea'. Kieran came up with a most inventive one:

'Died In A Rolls Royce Having Over-eaten Again.'

His friend devised a rather ruder version:

'Dash In A Real Rush, Help Or Exploding Arse.'

I suggested he might amend it slightly to 'Dash In A Real Rush, Help Or Else Accident', but perhaps it is not quite as memorable.

On a teachers' course I asked the delegates to think up their own mnemonic. One woman suggested a somewhat rude aide-mémoire:

'Do It At Robert Redford's House On Every Afternoon.'

A last note on this word that so many people find difficult to spell. A very large woman arrived at a school and climbed up a long flight of stairs to the second floor, out of breath, having found the climb exhausting.

"Ah've come to tell thee that our Shane wain't be in t' scoil today," she panted, "'cos 'e's got diarrhoea."

The school secretary thanked her, but pointed out she could have saved her the trouble of calling in by sending a note.

The mother's reply was short and blunt.

"Look, love," she told her, "does tha think that I'd 'ave climbed all these ruddy stairs if I could spell diarrhoea?"

SALOMÉ DANCED NAKED BEFORE HARRODS

Classroom 'howlers'

In one school I visited, the teachers had the good grace to laugh at themselves and appreciate that even they make gaffes when it comes to this tricky and troublesome language of ours.

In the school magazine were printed the usual assortment of howlers from the pupils but also a selection from the teachers.

For example, there was the instruction from the maths teacher on the geometry paper that "this option is compulsory", and the question posed by his history colleague on the history paper: "Trace the events leading up to the birth of James I".

Teachers (myself included) are not above sometimes making a gaffe when it comes to the language.

A primary teacher asked the children in her class to complete the worksheet headed 'Draw and describe a Roman soldier you know well'; another wrote on a five-year-old child's school report that "Thomas tends to be very immature at times". On another infant school report the teacher had written: "Beccy can read well and already knows a number of four-letter words."

An English teacher's report stated that "John's reading accuracy score would have been improved if he had read more accurately"; and a science teacher complained in his report: "Debbie's work is spoilt by dirty drawings."

One deputy head teacher admitted to shouting in assembly:

"Every time I open my mouth some very silly person speaks!"

Even head teachers slip up sometimes. A primary school head teacher placed a notice on the staffroom noticeboard in winter:

"Children must not skate on the frozen water unless passed by the head."

Another, commenting on the fire which destroyed the science block, announced:

"This is the worst disaster for the school since I was appointed."

Speaking after the election of the new chair of governors of a large comprehensive school, a headmaster declared:

"I have to say that we couldn't get anybody better."

The chair of governors at a speech day informed the parents and their pupils that the inspection report on the school had, in his opinion, been unfairly critical.

"When we read it," he said, "the headmaster and I felt we were standing on the edge of a precipice." He continued, "However, we are moving forward with confidence."

At another speech day, the chair of governors invited the school chaplain "to lead us in a few words of silent prayer".

Parents, too, are sometimes unintentionally amusing in their use of language. One mother, having been asked by the school if her son was "a natural-born British subject", replied that he was born by caesarean section; another, asked for her length of residence, informed the school:

"It's about thirty feet but I'm not that sure."

The more important the person making a blunder, the more enjoyable it is for those who witness it. The former Chief Inspector of Schools, charged with driving up standards, sent out a press release under this heading:

"School Inpsection [sic] Outcome Figures."

Here is a selection of pupil howlers:

Elijah went to Heaven in a fiery carrot.

Q. Name the Romans' greatest achievement.
A. Learning to speak Latin.

Q. What are steroids?
A. Things that stop the carpet slipping on the stairs.

Q. What is artificial insemination?
A. It's when the farmer does it instead of the bull.

Q. What is a seizure?
A. A Roman emperor.

Q. What guarantees may a mortgage company insist upon?
A. That the customer is well-endowed.

Q. What is a terminal illness?
A. When someone is ill at the airport.

Q. What is a fibula?
A. A small lie.

Q. What is a Caesarean Section?
A. A district in Rome.

Q. What is artificial respiration commonly known as?
A. The kiss of death.

Q. The Isle of Man is noted for which dangerous race?
A. The Vikings.

Q. Why do we have elections in a democratic society?
A. Because if men didn't have them they couldn't produce children.

Barbarians are the small metal balls which help machines run smoothly.

Q. What word describes a person who keeps on going despite difficulties?
A. Passionate.

Q. What was Hitler's secret weapon?
A. He used the dreaded Gaspacho.

Romeo's last wish was to be laid by Juliet.

The appearance of the anus in evolution was a massive breakthrough.

Young people sometimes, of course, deliberately misuse language for comic effect. Here are few intentional faux pas:

Q. What do you do when you come to a full stop?
A. Get off the bus.

Q. What is Baden-Powell connected with?
A. A hyphen.

Q. Where is Hadrian's Wall?
A. Around Hadrian's garden.

Q. What is the opposite of 'woe'?
A. Giddy up!

Q. Name a big bird with a long neck.
A. Naomi Campbell.

Q. What advice would you give to someone handling dangerous chemicals?
A. Be very very careful.

Q. What does the Bible say about those who live by the sword?
A. That they will get shot by those who have a gun.

Use a bum St Bernard to heat the test tube.

Q. How can you delay turning milk sour?
A. Keep it in the cow.

Q. What is the capital of Spain?
A. The letter 'S'.

Q. If a mother had three children but only two potatoes and wanted to give each child an equal share, how could she do it?
A. Mash the potatoes.

Crabs are crushed Asians.

One way the Jews and Arabs can settle the crisis in the Middle East is to sit down and discuss things like good Christians.

Milton wrote *Paradise Lost*. Then his wife died and he wrote *Paradise Regained*.

Joan of Arc was condomed to death.

Salomé danced naked before Harrods.

The pelvis protects the gentiles.

The sickle on the Russian flag stands for chopping people's heads off.

The life of a frog is extremely boring but they get used to it.

I recall when I was at school in the geography GCE class with Mr Schofield, Simon Watson had brought in a particularly unusual-looking lump of rock his father had discovered in Derbyshire.

"Sir," asked the pupil, "do you know what sort of rock this is?"

John Trollop, the wit of the class (and there always seems to be a class comedian), announced:

"Why it's sedimentary my dear Watson."

"I REPRESENT THE ACCUSATION THAT I'M LIVING OFF IMMORTAL EARNINGS."

Gaffes in the courtroom

Judges and lawyers, despite their erudition and knowledge of the legal system, sometimes say the most extraordinary things.

The prosecuting counsel, Mervyn Griffith-Jones, at the trial of the publisher of *Lady Chatterley's Lover* in 1960, caused much amusement in court when he asked the jury: "Is it a book that you would have lying around your house? Is it a book that you would even wish your wife or your servants to read?"

More recently, Judge John Garavan sympathised with the plight of a refugee who faced a second conviction for shoplifting with the comment that "If one is completely deprived it must be impossible not to be tempted to steal".

In another ill-advised remark, when hearing for an application for an extension of a nightclub, His Honour observed:

"I hear from respectable young men that they can't meet nice respectable girls in these nightclubs. The girls they meet are dreadful."

Judge Garavan was not averse to imparting some words on the subject of love to a young man who told the court he had committed the crime because he had his girlfriend on his mind.

"With spring coming up, you'd want to watch it," the judge advised, "because a young man's thoughts turn to things in spring that young women have been thinking about all winter."

My good friend the lawyer Stephen W Smith recounts in his books (*Boozers, Ballcocks and Bail* and *Fiddlers, Fakers and Fleas*) many anecdotes about the amusing side of the legal profession.

My favourite story is of the young man accused of stealing two shoes — both for the right foot, one size eleven, the other size nine. As most of us are aware, shoe shops, wishing to discourage theft, only display shoes which fit the right foot. The youth was caught limping through the town centre; he was arrested, charged and appeared later before the visiting district judge. The courtroom exchanges went something like this:

> Judge (to defence counsel): Is the man employed?
>
> Defence Counsel: I think not, your honour.
>
> Judge: Is he on benefits?
>
> Defence Counsel (to accused): Are you on benefits?
>
> Accused (to defence counsel): What?
>
> Defence Counsel (to accused): Are you in receipt of any benefits?
>
> Accused (to defence counsel): What?
>
> Defence Counsel (to accused): Are you on anything?
>
> Accused (to defence counsel): None of your business.
>
> Defence Counsel (to accused): The judge wishes to know if you are on anything.
>
> Accused (to defence counsel): I smoke a bit of weed now and again.
>
> Defence Counsel (to accused): I'm talking about benefits. What benefit do you receive?
>
> Accused (to defence counsel): It makes me happy.
>
> Defence Counsel (to judge): I think my client is on incapacity benefit, your honour.

Here are a few more classic courtroom gaffes:

Prosecution Counsel: Now doctor, and are you entirely certain that the man was dead when you carried out the autopsy?

Witness: Yes.

Prosecution Counsel: You are certain?

Witness: I am.

Prosecution Counsel: No doubt in your mind?

Witness: None.

Prosecution Counsel: Did you check for a pulse?

Witness: No.

Prosecution Counsel: Did you listen for a heartbeat?

Witness: No.

Prosecution Counsel: Did you ascertain if he was breathing?

Witness: No.

Prosecution Counsel: So, let me get this right. You did not check for pulse, heartbeat or breathing?

Witness: That is correct.

Prosecution Counsel: Then how can you say with certainty that the man was not alive?

Witness: Because his brain had been removed.

Prosecution Counsel: So, he could not have been alive?

Witness: Well, he might be alive and practising law somewhere not too far from here.

Defence Counsel: And what did your husband do before you married him?

Witness: A lot of things he didn't tell me about.

Judge: And he was hit in the fracas?

Witness: No, your honour, on the head.

Woman accused of prostitution: "I represent the accusation that I am living off of immortal earnings."

Defence Counsel: Were you hit in the fracas?
Witness: No, on the head.

Prosecution Counsel: Are you in a sexual relationship with the accused?

Witness: I refuse to answer that question.

Prosecution Counsel: Have you spent the night with him?

Accused: I refuse to answer that question.

Prosecution Counsel: Is it not the case that you are he are lovers?

Accused: Yes.

Judge: I take it that your appearance in court this morning is on the advice of your solicitor?

Witness: Yes, he told me to dress like this.

Prosecution Counsel: And you saw him pick the cat up and swing it around?

Witness: Yes I did.

Prosecution Counsel: You saw him pick the cat up and swing it around by its tail?

Witness: Yes.

Prosecution Counsel: And where was the cat at the time?

Witness: Attached to its tail.

Chairman of the Tribunal: You are Professor J Macdonald Fric?

Witness: No.

Chairman of the Tribunal: You are not Professor J Macdonald Fric?

Witness: That is correct.

Chairman of the Tribunal: Well who are you?

Witness: I am Professor J Macdonald, Fellow of the Royal Institute of Chemists.

'NEW RESEARCH INTO CAUSES OF DYSEXLIA'

Newspapers and magazines

Newspapers offer a rich source of gaffes, misprints, grammatical errors, solecisms, ambiguities and misquotes. I do feel, however, a certain sympathy for the journalist, for he or she has a deadline to meet and hasn't the luxury of the author who can read and re-read the text at leisure, and then have an editor and proofreader to check over what has been written.

As a contributor to a number of newspapers and journals and in a rush to meet the deadline, I have certainly made my fair share of blunders.

I was once taken to task by a reader of the *Yorkshire Post* when I mentioned in an article that certain things — litter, chewing gum on pavements, rude people, loud music — aggravated me. He pointed out that I should have used 'irritate' or 'displease', for 'aggravate' means 'to increase the gravity of an illness — one aggravates a wound.' He is right. To use the word in the sense of 'annoy' or 'exasperate' is regarded as incorrect by some traditionalists on the grounds that it is too radical a departure from the etymological meaning of 'to make heavy' (from the Latin *aggravare*). The *Oxford English Dictionary* states that the word, which dates back to the seventeenth century, "is in widespread use in modern English to mean 'annoy' but is still regarded as incorrect by some traditionalists." In my defence I did point out to my reader that 'aggravate' is comparable to meaning changes in hundreds of others words which have long been accepted without comment and that the Collins dictionary states that it is often used informally to mean 'to annoy, exasperate, especially a persistent goading'.

I am grateful for the editors who check over the manuscripts for my books. When I submitted the manuscript to the Dalesman of my book *Gervase Phinn's Yorkshire Journey*, Mark, my editor, pointed out the following misprints:

"I once accompanied a school party around the vast cathedral at York. The teacher and her class of seven and eight year olds stood in the centre of the great cathedral. They all stared in wonder at the largest medieval widow in Europe, the size of a double tennis court."

and

"Some of England's fiercest and bloodiest encounters have been fought on the flat land around here, decisive ballets like Stamford Bridge, Towton and Marston Moor to name but three."

I blamed the spill-chucker!

Seeing the words displayed in large black capitals on boards outside newsagents or as the headlines to newspaper articles, I sometimes wonder if those writers are deliberately trying to be witty and ambiguous to be eye-catching, or if the composer is just unaware of just how amusing such headlines can be.

Man At Death's Door — Doctors Pull Him Through.

Save Our Trees — They Break Wind.

Man Battered in Fish Shop. Youth Jailed for Assault.

New Research into the Causes Of Dysexlia.

Maths Teacher Suspended by Head.

Golfer Charged with Drunken Driving.

Crash Course for New Drivers.

Pupils Cut to Ease Crowding.

Iraqi Head Seeks Arms.

Schizophrenic Kills Herself with Two Plastic Bags.

Open Bowels Festival a Great Success.

Panda Mating Fails! Veterinarian Takes Over.

Red Tape Holds up New Bridge.

Stiff Opposition to New Crematorium.

Leopard Spotted In Park.

Spider Found in Toilet. Woman Relieved.

Headmistress Unveils Bust.

Boxer Hopes Past is Behind Him.

Half of Children in Town Below Average.

'Body In Garden is a Plant' says Woman.

Prince Charles Paying a Surprise Visit on Thursday.

I guess the writers of these paragraphs were also unaware of the perceived double meanings:

The skull of a Neanderthal man is displayed in the National Museum. There are only two such specimens in existence. Professor Thackeray has the other one.

It was reported that as a result of spending cuts in education, the plans to build the new library would have to be shelved.

It was felt that mentioning academic requirements on job advertisements might deter candidates with poorer qualifications.

Prospective candidate Mrs Iona Smithson said that her experience teaching children with special educational needs has given her the right kind of experience to represent residents.

Newspapers are full of misquotations and misprints. Here are some unintended examples:

> The ladies of the Merry Oldsters enjoyed a swap social on Friday evening. Everybody brought along something they no longer needed. Many ladies brought their husbands with them.

> What is Hell really like? Come and hear our guest speaker, the Reverend Marchbanks, next Sunday.

> Arthur Kitchener was seriously burned on Saturday when he came in contact with a high-voltage wife.

> Londonderry Development Commission plans to spend about £25,000 on improving the standard of street fighting in the city centre.

> The skeleton was believed to be that of a Saxon worrier.

> What is behind Red Nose Day? See Pick of the Week.

> A transplant surgeon has called for a ban on 'kidneys-for-ale' operations.

With such faux pas there come the corrections and clarifications:

> We apologise to Dr Charlocks. Reference to the "bust clinic" referred to in the article which appeared on September 8th should have read "busy clinic".

> In some of our copies of the article 'The Power of the Papacy' the Pope is described as "His Satanic Majesty". It should have read "The Roman Antichrist".
> (*Protestant Telegraph*)

> We apologise to Mr J J Thomson for the printing error which appeared in the letter advertising the Old Boys'

Dinner. It referred to him as 'an old waster' and should, of course have read 'an old master'.

In a recent report of a competition held in one of Pontin's holiday camps it was inadvertently stated that it was for elephant grandmothers instead of elegant grandmothers. We apologise for Mrs Helen P---- who gained third place, for any embarrassment this may have caused.

We apologise for the error in last week's paper in which we described Mr Steven B----- as "a former defective in the police force". It should have read "a former detective in the police farce".

We stated in an inquest report on Saturday that Mrs Susannah V----- of Porth was found dead with a bottle in her left hand and a plastic bag over her head. This should have read "a Bible in her left hand".

In last week's obituary column we mistakenly reported that General F--- was a bottle-scarred hero. We apologise for the error. We obviously meant that he was a battle-scared hero.

Advertisements in newspapers and journals frequently bring a smile to one's face:

Are you going places in aluminium foil?

The management is looking for a mature person to cook.

Elizabeth Arden has attractive openings.

Machine Tool Manufacturer requires male parts handler.

Women to pick fresh fruit and produce by night.

Experienced butcher required. Able to cut, skewer and serve the customers.

An opportunity to join an expanding contracting company.

Honest and reliable worker seeks work. Will take anything.

Stud farm requires fit young man.

Wanted: part-time kitchen assistant. Must be willing to get hands dirty.

Required for September, a qualified and experienced three years old teacher for pre-school.

The successful candidate must have the proven ability to demonstrate the facility to exhibit a range of excellent communication skills.

Teacher of Geography required. The capacity to teach Geography will be an advantage.

Proof-reader required. Must have high level of accurracy.

There is a permanent position for a Yoga Instructor.

And finally, there are display advertisements and the small ads:

Dont kill your wife with hard work — let electricity do it for you!

Doberman puppy for sale. Eats anything. Fond of children.

For sale: Braille dictionary. Must be seen to be appreciated.

Guillotine wanted for playgroup.

Do you scratch your bottom whilst taking a bath? Have it re-glazed by the professional.

Hearse for sale. Body in need of some attention.

Ford Mondeo. W reg. good condition. Taxed. MOT. Radio. £2.240 ono. Phone 743660 after 6pm.
Ford Escort. 2009, low mileage, one owner, service history, air conditioning, VGC, £3,499. Phone 759467.
Ford, Brian. Died 21st December, loving husband and father. Sadly missed.

ESCHATOLOGICAL INEXACTITUDES

Unusual words

Ilove this rich, poetic, tricky, troublesome, inconsistent language of ours. Since an early age (and on the advice of my brilliant English teacher Kenneth Pike) I have written down words in my notebook which have unusual spellings, ones which I have never come across before and those which simply appeal to me. I have lists of them. Here are some of my favourites:

hobbledehoy	ragamuffin	brouhaha
autochthonous	esurient	lucubration
prescience	swashbuckling	dandified
deracinated	troublous	inspissated
monody	propinquity	nonchalance
haecceity	ptarmigan	viscosity
weasel	pontificate	avuncular
contrapuntal	expostulatory	harridan
gewgaws	bellicose	

Shakespeare was the first recorded user of about two thousand words of which nearly half have now, sadly, fallen out of use. We continue to use 'abhorred', 'abstemious' and 'accessible', but we have lost some wonderful words like 'adoptious', 'abidance',

"To clarify, I would classify that as an
eschatological inexactitude."

'allayment' and 'annexment'. He was a great one for inventing words, too, was the 'Bard of Avon'.

Like Shakespeare, some people still love to create new words and expressions, words that don't exist in the language but the inventor thinks they ought to.

Connie, the cleaner at the teachers' centre, was greatly adept at this.

"Mr Phinn," she once said to me, "you're so artificated."

On another occasion she saw a colleague waving at me madly from across the office and pointing to the ringing telephone.

"Mr Smith's testiculating," she told me.

The *Sunday Times* conducted a survey to discover what people thought were the most beautiful words in the English language. Here is the top ten:

melody/velvet	gossamer/crystal	autumn
peace	tranquil	twilight
murmur	caress	mellifluous
whisper		

When readers were asked to list the words they hated most, those with unpleasant connotations were obvious choices:

gizzard	slop	carbuncle
scrawny	ganglion	insipid
tyrannical	incarcerate	haemorrhaging
bulbous	slimy	snot
clot	prig	

It is understandable that words that bring on nausea like 'vomit', 'gobbet', 'sputum' and 'scum' were high on the list but there were some idiosyncratic and sometimes surprising offerings. These included 'gusset', 'hubby', 'panties', 'poppet' and (predictably from the two teachers who wrote) the acronym OFSTED.

Poets at the Ledbury Literary Festival were asked which word they thought was the ugliest in the language.

Geraldine Monk disliked the word 'redacted' (to have written out in literary form or edited for publication), a word I have to admit I had never come across.

"It's a brutish-sounding word," she said. "It doesn't flow, it prods at you in a nasty manner."

Philip Wells had an intense dislike of the word 'pulchritude' (which paradoxically means 'beautiful'). Wells was vehement in his aversion to the word.

"It violates all the magical impulses of balanced onomatopoeic language," he said, "being stuffed to the brim with a brutally Latinate cudgel of barbaric consonants."

Wow! That's a bit strong. Actually, I quite like saying the word. It's from Middle English and fallen out of use. I think it should be more commonly used, particularly the adjectival form of 'pulchritudinous.'

I met Hilary Murphy on a cruise ship. She was on the front row for one of my lectures on English spelling, and was willing with some of the audience (but not all) to have a go at a spelling test.

"Anyone who gets them all right," I said, confident in the knowledge that none would, "I will give to him or her a signed first-edition copy of my latest book."

Hilary not only spelled the thirty words correctly but gave me a list of other tricky words. I was amazed by her knowledge and then discovered that it is she who sets the questions on the popular quiz TV show Who Wants to be a Millionaire?. I am indebted to Hilary for these wonderfully expressive words and their meanings:

aleatory	depending on the throw of the dice
bibulous	addicted to alcohol
borborygmus	rumbling of gas in the intestine

cicatrization	healed by the forming of a scar
defenestration	throwing a person out of a window
ergophobia	dread of work
excoriate	peel off, strip, remove skin by abrasion
gallimoufry	jumble, medley
glabrous	bald, completely smooth
gnomon	the rod of a sundial
picayune	insignificant thing or person
steatopygic	having excess fat on the buttocks
teratogenic	producing monsters
uxorious	fondness for one's wife
fusticate	to beat with a stick
galeathropy	the delusion that you have become a cat
umbrageous	offensive, annoying
epithalamium	poem or song celebrating marriage
coriaceous	like leather
rachitic	suffering from rickets
eirenic	aiming for peace
turgescence	swelling
senescent	deteriorating with age
logorrhoea	an excessive flow of words

Being a nosy sort of person, I asked Hilary what was the most memorable moment on Who Wants to be a Millionaire?. A contestant, she told me, was asked the question:

"The Archbishop of Canterbury is known as a ...?"

There were four options: 'primate', 'marsupial', 'mammal' and 'rodent'.

The contestant opted to go 'fifty-fifty' and was given two choices of 'primate' and 'marsupial'.

"I'll phone a friend," said the contestant.

The friend — yes, you have guessed — opted for 'marsupial'. Whenever I see the smiling face and shining eyes of Justin Welby on the television screen, I cannot think of him as being anything other than 'The Marsupial of All England'.

Recently I went to buy a mouse (that little gadget plugged into my computer to help me move the cursor about). At the shop I was in a dilemma — was it 'two mice' or 'two mouses'? The helpful assistant informed me the correct term was 'mouses', "So we don't get confused with those little furry creatures," he told me. One wonders why I would go into PC World to buy a rodent.

The word 'mouses' is a neologism — one of these newly-coined words that have entered our linguistic consciousness.

Newly-invented words enter the language all the time. In the sixteenth century, neologisms — "smelling too much of the Latin" as the poet Richard Willes put it — were frowned upon by many. Willes took particular exception to the following words which are now perfectly acceptable and appear in the dictionary: 'portentous', 'antiques', 'despicable', 'obsequious', 'homicide', 'destructive' and 'prodigious'.

In the nineteenth century, the English poet William Barnes was still fighting the battle to eradicate such foreign aberrations as 'preface' and 'photograph' which, he suggested, should be renamed 'foreword' and 'sun print' in order to achieve proper Englishness. 'Foreword' is now an acceptably-used word; 'sun print', however, never caught on.

One word I do find rather ugly is 'galimatias'. It sounds like a disease of a very personal nature or a species of parasitical plant. However, it is a word which those who use that management terminology which infects the language like bacilli should know. It means a style of writing which is confused and full of some-what meaningless jargon. I shall come on to that in the next chapter...

UNKNOWN UNKNOWNS ARE THE ONES WE DON'T KNOW WE DON'T KNOW

Buzzwords, jargon and gobbledegook

> No public business of any kind could possibly be
> done at any tine without the acquiescence of the
> Circumlocution Office. Its finger was in the
> largest public pie and the smallest public tart.
> (Charles Dickens, *Little Dorritt*)

Buzzwords are fashionable or vogue words which have crept
invidiously into the language. They are designed to make the
speaker (sorry, 'facilitator') sound go-ahead, up-to-date, something of a specialist. Many come from the world of business and
from computer technology. The word itself relates chiefly to 'buzz'
in the sense of being excited or purposeful.

I wince when listening to a lecture on management where
the speaker employs the latest trendy words and phrases.

I particularly bristle when I am exhorted to 'run that extra
mile', 'give it 110%', 'get on board', 'suck it and see', 'bounce ideas
around', 'throw it into the ring', 'pull in the same direction' or
'give it my best shot'.

I dislike having things 'flagged up' for me and I don't feel
inclined to 'get up to speed', 'think outside the box', 'climb
aboard', 'push the envelope' and 'find a window in my diary'.

I don't want to 'touch base,' 'drill down to it', 'cross-pollinate

"As I'm the inter-departmental meetings facilitator, I would ask everyone who is already up to speed to throw their idea-hats into the ring so we can run them up the flagpole to see who salutes; that way, we'll all be pulling in the same direction to square the circle with the aim of actioning this vertical approach for each objective. Is that clear?"

across your demographic', 'run it up the flagpole to see who salutes', 'square the circle', 'action this kind of vertical approach on every platform' or engage in 'blue-sky thinking'.

I do not like 'no-brainers' and 'bullet points', and I don't want to 'chill out' or 'have a comfort break'.

Buzzwords reveal nothing that couldn't be more effectively communicated using simple language. There are ample words in English to express one's feelings clearly and accurately without resorting to this twaddle.

Gobbledegook is a word which was invented by the Texan lawyer Maury Maverick to describe the convoluted, pretentious and often meaningless language of bureaucracy. Asked in an interview for the *New York Times* how he thought of the word, Maverick explained that he coined 'gobbledegook' when he was thinking of "the old bearded turkey gobbler who was always gobble-gobbling and strutting with ludicrous pomposity. At the end of this gobble there was a sort of gook."

Never has so much has been said and meant so little.

The Ministry of Defence produced this classic amendment to what deserves to be a top-secret document. It reads:

> 'Quote, Page 10, Para 16c, second line, insert quote in unquote between quote and unquote and quote the unquote.'

Here are a few classics from education:

> 'In pursuance of section 4(3) of the Education Act of 1980, this Instrument shall have effect subject to any provision in the regulations from time to time in force under 4(1) of the Education Act of 1980, and any reference in this Instrument to the Regulations so in force. Any reference in this Instrument to a paragraph is a reference to that paragraph thereof and any reference in a paragraph to a

sub-paragraph is a reference to a sub-paragraph in that paragraph.'
(Special Schools – Instrument of Government)

'I must emphasise that the remedial teams are language teaching practitioners whose task is to work alongside the teachers in the classroom. They are not merely a pair of hands to listen to children read.'
(From a circular to schools)

'This basic course in child abuse is intended for workers who have little experience in child abuse and wish to acquaint themselves with the procedures and practices.'
(In-service handbook for teachers)

'Does the practice of international politics tell us more about international theory than the dominant debates within international theory can tell us about international politics?'
(Question on university examination paper)

'Candidates will be considered for this post with a proven record of coordinating a major subject discipline in the school. We are aware of the inaccuracies of our appointment system so if you feel you cannot match the job specification, please do not apply as you might be appointed.'
(Advertisement for a deputy head teacher's post in a middle school)

'It has come to my attention that there may be some slight confusion over what constitutes a living individual for the purpose of registration under the Act, insofar as systems are concerned. I wish therefore to reiterate that this category includes all living individuals, pupils included.'
(Advice on the Data Protection Act)

'There is no formal link between the content of the
activities and skills triplets targeted.'
(AQA Guidance on Setting the Centre-Assessed
Component)

'High-quality learning environments are a necessary
precondition for facilitation and enhancement of the
on-going learning processes children need in good schools.'
(From a circular to schools)

To researchers at St Andrew's University redesigning the
keyboard on smartphones, the traditional QWERTY keyboard
isn't just a keyboard; it's a 'suboptimal text entry interface'.

When Education Secretary Michael Gove was responding to
critics of David Cameron's leadership, he commented that
"The idea of changing the leader is bonkerooney".

US presidential candidate Mitt Romney's baffling observation
when 'on the stump' must rank as one of the best examples of
gobbledegook:

"I believe in an America where millions of Americans
believe in an America that Americans believe in. That's
the America I love."

Here is fellow American politician Donald Rumsfeld with an
equally baffling explanation:

"Reports that say that something hasn't happened are always
interesting to me, because as we know, there are known
knowns; there are things we know we know. We also know
there are known unknowns; that is to say we know there
are some things we do not know. But there are unknown
unknowns — the ones we don't know we don't know."

THE WRITING'S ON THE WALL

Graffiti

Any inscription or drawing scratched or carved onto a surface especially a wall is graffito. Originally the name applied to the wall scribblings found at Pompeii and other Roman towns and cities.

The plural graffiti (from the Italian *graffito* meaning 'a little scratch') now usually describes messages scribbled on the walls of public toilets and advertising posters, and sometimes emblazoned on the front of seaside T-shirts or displayed in car rear view windows.

Some examples of graffiti are witty and satirical such as the one seen in Manchester which read

'If you hate graffiti, sign a partition'
or the writing beneath the sign

'Mersey Docks and Harbour Board'
which read

'And little lambs eat ivy.'
Sometimes such wall scribblings are obscene and highly offensive, others downright ridiculous, and some are witty and satirical, but there are ways of laughing at the silly instructions, pompous statements and pretentious notices. Here are a few of my favourite examples:

'Stop Global Whining.'

'Where there's a whip, there's a way.'

'Get it done by Friday'
stated the notice on an office wall. Underneath, someone
had written:
'signed, Robinson Crusoe.'

'Don't use a long word where a diminutive one will suffice.'

'If at first you don't succeed, skydiving is not for you.'

'A turkey is not just for Christmas, it's for Boxing Day as
well.'

'All work and no play makes you a manager.'

'Princess sick of prince seeks frog.'

'Be nice to your children. They'll choose your nursing home.'

'Grow your own dope. Plant a man.'

'Never fall for a tennis player. Love means nothing to him.'

'If tomorrow never comes then you are dead.'

'Rehab is for quitters.'

'If you always smile when things go wrong then you have
someone in mind to blame.'

'Coffee, chocolate and men: some things are better rich.'

'Old age is always fifteen years older than I am.'

Written underneath the recruiting poster which read
'The Army Builds Men'
were the words
'Build one for me please – Tracey.'

Underneath a poster advertising an air show
'The Red Arrows Flying Display'
someone had written
'If wet, in the village hall.'

PTO ASAP FOR CBOH & POETS WHEN YOYO

Abbreviations

In every walk of life — be it education, medicine, business, commerce or advertising — abbreviations pepper documents. Some are ones with which we are familiar — AOB, PTO, CV, TA, PhD, WC, MA, RSVP — but some are coded messages only understood by those in the know.

The medical profession has a variety of abbreviations used by the doctors and nurses but, thankfully, meaningless to most patients, also known as ODSA (Original Doctors' Shorthand Acronyms):

AGA	Acute Gravity Attack (ie, the patient fell over)
AITM	All In The Mind
AMA	Against Medical Advice
AOB	Alcohol On Breath
AWTF	Away With The Fairies
BIBA	Brought In By Ambulance
BID	Brought In Dead
BVA	Breathing Valuable Air
BWS	Beached Whale Syndrome
CBOH	Clean Bill Of Health

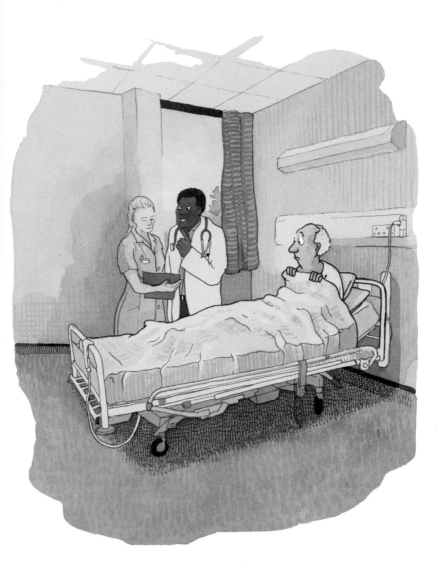

"This patient was BIBA with AGA but AMA was given CBOH
and is PITB so DTMA, OK?"

CTD	Close To Death *or* Circling The Drain
DBI	Dirt Bag Index (multiply the number of tattoos by the number of teeth to work out how many days since the patient has bathed)
DAFO	Drunk And Fell Over
DOA	Drunk *or* Dead On Arrival
DTMA	Don't Transfer to Me Again
DTS	Danger To Shipping
FLK	Funny Looking Kid
FLKFLP	Funny Looking Kid, Funny Looking Parents
GOMER	Get Out of My Emergency Room
GROLIES	*Guardian* Reader Of Low Intelligence in Ethnic Skirt
HBD	Has Been Drinking
HIVI	Husband Is Village Idiot
LOLNAD	Little Old Lady with No Actual Disease
LOBNH	Lights On But Nobody Home
MAAH	Mad As A Hatter
MTTT	More Tattoos Than Teeth
OAP	Over-Anxious Parent *or* On Another Planet
PGT	Patient Got Thumped
PISA	Permanent & Irrecoverable State of Alcoholism
PITB	Pain In The Bum
PP	Plumbums Pendulums (sham Latin for 'swinging the lead')
PVN	Patient Very Nervous
TEETH	Tried Everything Else, Try Homeopathy
UBI	Unexplained Beer Injury

Those who work in offices also have their own secret codes:

ACU	Another Cock-Up
AFC	Away From Computer
BIIT	Boss Is In Today
CYB	Cover Your Back
DSTM	Don't Shoot The Messenger
FYI	For Your Information
JFDI	Just Flipping Do It
OFINTOT	Oh Flip I Never Thought Of That
PICNIC	Problem In Chair Not In Computer
PLMK	Please Let Me Know
POETS	Push Off Early, Tomorrow's Saturday
TMI	Too Much Information
TPTB	The Powers That Be
TGIF	Thank God It's Friday
WFH	Working From Home
WOS	Waste Of Space
WRS	Work-Related Stress
YOYO	You're On Your Own

When I started teaching in 1970 there was the DES (Department of Education and Science), which became the DfEE (Department for Education and Employment), then the DfES (Department for Education and Schools). Then came the DfCSF (the Department for Children, Schools and Families), known to teachers as the Department for Curtains and Soft Furnishings and to the more cynical in the profession as the Department for Comedy and Science Fiction. Now we have the DfE (Department for Education). No doubt the next Government will think up yet another abbreviation.

SEALS BOGOF
FOR EUREKA
Acronyms and bacronyms

An acronym (from the Greek *akros* meaning 'outermost' and *onoma* meaning 'name') is a word formed from the initial letter of a group of connected words and pronounced as a word, such as NIMBY (Not in my back yard), BOGOFF (Buy one get one for free), SWALK (Sealed with a loving kiss) and ERNIE (Electronic Random Number Indicator Equipment).

The acronym likely to put the fear of God into head teachers and teachers is, of course, the dreaded OFSTED (Office for Standards in Education).

A recent tendency is for the names of certain organisations, movements and charities to spell out an expressive or punning acronym rather than a meaningless word. Here are some rather inventive examples:

SMART	Special Measures Action Reform Team
SEALS	Sea, Air and Land Service
STEP	Special Temporary Employment Programme
CHIME	Churches' Initiative in Musical Education
EUREKA	European Research Cooperation Agency
ADAPT	Access for Disabled People to Art Today

"Bogoff, mummy, bogoff!"

I was once told by a member of the teaching staff that she was a PRAT. I felt her to be rather hard on herself until she explained she was the Peripatetic Remedial Advisory Teacher.

Nowadays the old social definitions like 'upper class' and 'working class' have been replaced by a range of demographic acronyms:

FEATHER	Financially Enabled Adult Trying Hard to Evade Responsibility
GLAM	Greying, Leisured, Affluent, Married
HOPEFUL	Hard-up Old Person Expecting Full Useful Life
KIPPERS	Kids In Parents' Pockets Eroding Retirement Savings
LIFER	Lazy Ignorant Fool Expecting Retirement
NINJA	No Income, No Job or Assets
OINKY	One Income, No Kids Yet
ORCHID	One Recent Child, Heavily In Debt
ROMEO	Retired Old Men Enjoying Outings
RUB	Rich Urban Biker
SINBAD	Single Income, No Boyfriend And Desperate
SITCOM	Single Income, Two Children, Outrageous Mortgage
SKI-ing	Spending Kids' Inheritance
SLOP	Single, Living Off Parents
WOOPie	Well-Off Older Person

During the the Second World War, those serving in the armed forces used acronyms in their correspondence to their loved ones (usually written on the backs of envelopes) to evade censorhip:

SWALK	Sealed With A Loving Kiss
ITALY	I Trust And Love You

NORWICH	Knickers Off Ready When I Come Home
BURMA	Be Undressed Ready My Angel
SIAM	Sexual Intercourse At Midnight
HOLLAND	Hope Our Love Lasts And Never Dies
EGYPT	Eager to Grab Your Pretty Toes
EDINBURGH	Elated Darling, I'm Near, Book Usual Room, Grand Hotel

And from wives and girlfriends at home:

| CHIP | Come Home I'm Pregnant |

Similar to the acronym is the 'bacronym', where an acronym is devised to fit an existing word, usually a brand name, and more often than not for comic effect. The car industry is an excellent environment for bacronyms, as these examples show:

BENTLEY	Beautiful Engine, Needs to Last Endless Years
BSA	Best Scrap Available
FIAT	Feeble Italian Attempt at Transportation
FORD	Found On Rubbish Dump
HONDA	Had One, Never Did Again
KIA	Killed In Automobile
LADA	Life And Death Association
LOTUS	Lots Of Trouble, Usually Serious
MAZDA	Made At Zoo by Demented Apes
MG	Mostly in Garage
PEUGEOT	Poor Engine, Useless Gearbox, Every One Trouble
SAAB	Something's Always About to Break
SUBARU	Still Usable But All Rusted Underneath
TOYOTA	The One You Ought To Avoid

Equally imaginative are the acronymic alternatives for the names of airlines:

AIR INDIA	After I Return I'll Never Do It Again
ALITALIA	Aircraft Lands In Turin And Luggage In Ancona
BEA	Britain's Excuse for an Airline
BOAC	Better On A Camel
DELTA	Don't Expect Luggage To Arrive
EASYJET	Economy Airline Slows Your Journey Every Time
EL AL	Every Landing Always Late
KLM	Keeps Losing Money
QANTAS	Quite A Nice Trip, All Survived
SABENA	Such A Bad Experience, Never Again
TWA	The Worst Airline

I rather like the story of the speechwriter who, having worked for his politician boss for many years, was summarily sacked. It was the practice for the said politician to have all his speeches written for him. He would collect the speech a few minutes before addressing his audience, not having read through it. The disgruntled speechwriter composed his most witty and erudite final effort, and the politician, as usual, began to read the speech to a most appreciative audience. Then he came to the penultimate page.

"I should now like to make some very important points about which I feel very strongly," he read.

He turned over the paper. There in large letters was the acronym YOYO.

He looked in desperation at the speechwriter who was sitting smiling on the front row. He mouthed:

"You're On Your Own."

TAKE OFF TOP AND PUSH UP BOTTOM
Instructions and warnings

In this health and safety age it is important to warn the consumers of the potential dangers in using a particular product. Some of the instructions, however, are baffling, some ambiguous, some blindingly obvious, and others bizarre and sometimes downright silly:

> Generous rounded bottom, ideal for beating
> (on mixing bowl)

> Wash and dress before eating
> (on a lettuce)

> Not suitable for children aged 36 months or less
> (on a birthday card for a one year old)

> Do not microwave
> (on a bottle of champagne)

> Warning! Wearing this Superman outfit
> does not enable you to fly
> (on a child's dressing-up costume)

> When opened please keep in an upright position
> (on a carton of milk)

"Mmm, let me read the instructions:
'Take off top and push up bottom'!"

Not to be used as a hairdryer
(on a heat gun)

Do not use for drying pets
(in the manual for a microwave oven)

This packet may contain nuts
(on a packet of peanuts)

May be harmful if swallowed
(on a shipment of hammers)

Take off top and push up bottom
(on a lipstick)

For indoor and outdoor use only
(on a can of paint)

Do not iron clothes on body
(on a steam iron)

Do not expose to naked flame
(on a lighter)

Peel tomatoes by standing in boiling water
(in a recipe book)

Caution: Remove infant before folding for storage
(on a child's pushchair)

Serving suggestion: defrost first
(on a ready-to-eat meal packet)

Do not spray on a naked flame
(on can of aerosol)

Do not use orally after using rectally
(on a digital thermometer)

MATERNITY UNIT: PLEASE USE BACK ENTRANCE

Signs and notices

Standing on the railway station platform on a cold wet winter morning, I noticed the sign chalked on the blackboard outside the gentlemen's toilet which made me chuckle:

'Wet Floor! This is not an instruction.'

We are surrounded by a world of shop signs, public notices, posters, billboards, announcements and advertisements, some of which like the one quoted make us smile. Others amuse us in their unintentional efforts to warn or inform.

'PLEASE LEAVE HEATHER FOR ALL TO ENJOY' proclaimed a sign outside a Peak District information centre.

Some notices are baffling, others curious and some make no sense at all. Here is a selection of my favourite ambiguous, silly, puzzling and meaningless signs:

After break could staff please wash their mugs and stand upside down on the draining board
(on a staffroom noticeboard)

One hour photographs. Ready tomorrow.

For anyone who has children and doesn't know it, there is a day-care centre on the first floor.
(at a conference)

Open seven days a week and at weekends.

GBH Fitness Club.

Maternity Unit. Please use the back entrance.

Weight watchers should use the double doors at the rear of the building.

Playground fine for littering.

Seasonal toilet rolls sold here.

Bomber jackets half price.
(in a Belfast clothing shop)

The 07.38 train to London has been cancelled owing to non-cervical stock.

Automatic door — push to operate.
(in hotel reception)

Closed for official opening.

Lions please stay in the car.
(at a safari park)

Please go slowly round the bend.
(traffic sign)

Could the congregation please note that the bowl marked 'For the Sick' at the rear of the church is for monetary donations only.

This door must not be used as an entrance or exit.

Any person not putting litter in this bin will be fined.
(in a children's playground)

Slow workmen in road.

Toilet for sitting down customers only.
(in a café)

On Thursday at 5pm there will be a meeting of the
'Little Mothers Club'. All wishing to become
little mothers please meet the vicar in his study.
(in a church newsletter)

Warning! Guard dogs operate here.
(in a hospital car park)

Footpath unsuitable for pedestrians.

We can repair anything.
Please knock hard on the door as bell doesn't work.
(on a shop door)

We exchange anything — bicycles, washing machines etc.
Why not bring your wife along and get a great bargain?
(outside a junk shop)

Would the person who took the stepladder
please return it or further steps will be taken.
(in an office reception area)

Caution! Water on road when raining.

Friendly Self-Service.
(at a petrol station)

Welcome to our ool. There is no 'P' in it.
Please keep it that way.
(at a swimming pool)

All children travelling in this vehicle must be belted.
(on a school bus)

Torture Chamber unsuitable for wheelchair users.
(on a castle wall).

True Born Romany. Closed this weekend due to
unforeseen circumstances.
(on a promenade booth)

'Warning! Guard dogs operate here.'

Notice to Staff. On no account must hot bottoms
be placed on this worktop.
(in a café kitchen)

Bus Stop. No waiting.

Automatic washing machines: please remove all your
clothes when the light goes out.
(in a launderette)

Happy Hour — 5pm to 7pm.

Sign in shop selling musical instruments:
'Bach in ten minutes.'

Sign in a school cafeteria:
'Shoes are required to eat in the cafeteria.'
Underneath a wit had written:
'Socks can eat wherever they want.'

Dogs must be carried on the escalators.

'Tek Care! Lambs on t' road.'
(hand-written traffic sign in Wensleydale)

Toilet out of order. Please use the floor below.

The meeting of the road safety committee has been cancelled
due to the chairman being involved in a road accident.

Bargain basement upstairs.

Lord Curzon, when the Viceroy of India, was on one of his regal
tours of the country. He came to a village which welcomed him
with a great banner which stretched across the only street. It was
a gala day, but the sign read:
            'A GAL A DAY.'
'Yes, yes,' laughed the Viceroy, 'I quite agree.'

LOST IN TRANSLATION

English as expressed by the rest of the world

In his excellent article 'Postscript to a Language', Andrew Giffin reminds us that there are 5,000 languages in the world and a billion people can speak English in one form or another.

"Combine these two facts," he says, "and you are bound to have problems."

He gives many examples of how English lays booby traps for the unwary foreigner:

"Any language where an unassuming word like 'fly' signifies an annoying insect, a means of travel and a critical part of a gentleman's apparel, is obviously asking for problems.

"Consider, then, the plight of the poor foreigner who has to learn that in the English speaking world an alarm goes off when in fact it goes on.

"The word 'set' has 58 uses as a noun, 126 as a verb and 10 as a participle adjective.

"The word 'second' can mean next after first; a sixtieth part of a minute; an attendant in a dual or boxing match; and with exactly the same spelling be pronounced 'si-cond' as a temporary transfer to another appointment."

Pity the poor foreigners, then, trying to get to grips with English. They have to learn it three times: first its meaning; then how to pronounce it; then how to spell it. The likelihood is that they will come a cropper at each stage. This poem summarises the pitfalls:

Why English is So Hard

We'll begin with a box, and the plural is boxes;
But the plural of ox should be oxen, not oxes.
Then one fowl is goose, but two are called geese;
Yet the plural of moose should never be meese.
You may find a lone mouse or a whole lot of mice,
But the plural of house is houses, not hice.
If the plural of man is always called men,
Why shouldn't the plural of pan be called pen?
The cow in the plural may be cows or kine,
But the plural of vow is vows, not vine.
And I speak of a foot, and you show me your feet,
But I give you a boot — would a pair be called beet?
If one is a tooth and a whole set are teeth,
Why shouldn't the plural of booth be called beeth?
If the singular is this, and the plural is these,
Should the plural of kiss be nicknamed kese?
Then one may be that, and three may be those,
Yet the plural of hat would never be hose;
We speak of a brother, and also of brethren,
But though we say mother, we never say methren.
The masculine pronouns are he, his, and him,
But imagine the feminine she, shis, and shim!
So our English, I think you will all agree,
Is the trickiest language you ever did see.

Of course understanding depends a great deal on context, because some words which are spelt the same have different meanings and some are different parts of speech. This can of course be very confusing for those whose first language is not

English. When I taught the foreign students, I demonstrated this with a few sentences:

> The general decided to desert his dessert in the desert.
>
> The examiner had to subject the subject to a battery of tests in each subject.
>
> The artist saw a tear in his masterpiece and shed a tear.
>
> The dentist administered a number of injections to make the patient's gums number.
>
> The pupil was too close to the door to close it.
>
> The policeman said the insurance for the invalid was invalid.
>
> The stag does strange things when the does are present.
>
> When shot at, the dove dove into the bushes.
>
> The oarsmen had a row about who should row the boat.
>
> The dustman decided to refuse to take the refuse.
>
> The nurse wound the bandage around the patient's wound.
>
> The plumber took the lead in getting the lead.
>
> The auctioneer did not object to the object.
>
> The farmer decided to produce produce.
>
> He decided to present the present, for he thought that there was no time like the present.

Klaus, the industrious German student, was fascinated by these sentences, and by some of the poems and pieces of prose (many of which he learnt by heart) which I gave to the class to demonstrate the tricky nature of English:

> Whether the weather is fine
> Or whether the weather is not,

Whether the weather is cold
Or whether the weather is hot,
We'll weather the weather,
Whatever the weather
Whether we like it or not.

A rough-coated, dough-faced, thoughtful ploughman
strode through the streets of Scarborough; after falling
into a slough, he coughed and hiccoughed.

My family put me to shame when it comes to speaking another
language, for I have only English to speak of (or rather, with).
Christine, my wife, speaks French and German; my children
Richard and Elizabeth have a fair command of French, Matthew is
fluent in Japanese, and Dominic, who spent eight years in China,
is a confident user of Mandarin and speaks pretty good Spanish.

When Christine and I visited Dominic in Nanjing he took us
to a plush restaurant famous for its authentic Chinese cuisine.
It was housed in a former splendidly domed, Greek Orthodox
church. I scanned the menu, with the translations in English:

> Spicy fish head.
>
> Grilled intestine with onion.
>
> Braised knuckles.
>
> Sliced sinews.
>
> Marinated ox tripe.
>
> Duck chin.
>
> Frogs with garlic pot.
>
> Sliced bladder with soy sauce.

I finally settled for something called 'American extremity'. I have
no idea what I ate but it was delicious. I guess it won't be too long
before it appears on the shelves at Tesco.

This kind of word-by-word literal translation into English from Far East languages is sometimes known as 'Engrish'. Here are a few more examples I have spotted:

> The current is swift water is deep danger.
> No amusement performance water swimming.
> (Sign on riverbank)

> Black bear is large body shape carnivore. Because they simultaneously have extremely keen canine tooth could piercing, rends the meat and also have the flat teeth for crushing, and salivating plantation. So the diet is quiet, diverse source of food.
> (information board at zoo)

> Big Size Girl. Greater XL.
> For larger legs and buttocks of women wearing.
> (on women's tights)

> Jeans for Aggressive Woman.
> (clothes shop sign)

> Please keep chair on position & keep table cleaned after dying. Thanks for your corporation.
> (cafeteria sign)

> This production can enactment break time, study time, hair dressing time, stew time, sun edition time and so on. Replace battery when ever reading becomes dim and difficult.
> (instructions for a digital kitchen timer)

I recently returned from a week in Tenerife. Whenever abroad I am always interested in the ways in which foreigners try and get their heads around this problematic language of ours. In the toilet at the hotel in which we stayed was a large notice which read:

> 'In the event of fire evacuate immediately and leave the premise.'

Over the years on my travels abroad I have collected a fair number of amusing, inventive and ambiguous instructions and notices. Here are a few of my favourites:

> Special today — No ice-cream
> (Venice)

> We take your bags and we send them in all directions.
> (Sweden)

> A special cocktail for ladies with nuts.
> (Tokyo)

> If this is your first visit to Moscow you are welcome to it.
> (Russia)

> Specialist in women and other diseases.
> (Rome)

> English well talking.
> (Majorca)

> Our wines leave you nothing to hope for.
> (Lisbon)

> Drop your trousers here for best results.
> (Nanjing cleaners)

Oscar Wilde once said that 'we share everything with the Americans except the language.'

Here is former president George W Bush on proposed education reforms: "You teach a child to read and he or her will be able to pass a literacy test."

But my very favourite are the words reputedly said by David Edwards, head of the Joint National Committee on Language in the United States, answering a question about the necessity for a commercial nation to be multilingual.

"If English was good enough for Jesus Christ," he allegedly stated, "then it's good enough for me."

"SO WHAT DO I CARE, AND MY HEAD IS AS EMPTY AS AIR"

The worst of verse

"The function of the poet is to strip the idea of
triviality and the accidental, and to reclothe it
in beauty and concrete form."
Sir Arthur Quiller-Couch

Much has been written about the power, poignancy and the
beauty of poetry, that it is the most wonderful form of
language and that poets represent the world more accurately than
anyone else. Poetry is said to be the highest form of language,
in which poets like artists look carefully at their subjects and then
select the best words to describe them.

Thomas Gray in 'The Progress of Poesy' claimed that poems are
"thoughts that breathe and words that burn".

Vernon Scannell argued that "The purpose of poetry is not to
inform but to inflame."

Matthew Arnold believed that "Great poetry does undoubtedly
tend to form the soul and character; it tends to beget a love of
beauty and truth in alliance together."

Coleridge described the poet "as a man speaking to men of
his and their condition, in language which consists of the best
words in the best order, language used with the greatest possible
inclusiveness and power."

In this chapter we see 'poets' using words in the worst possible order, which are pretty much bereft of any power, poignancy or beauty, in language hardly likely to delight or to inflame.

Keats in a letter to John Taylor remarked:

"If poetry comes not as naturally as the leaves to a tree it had better not come at all."

Good advice which the poets here might well have been advised to heed before committing their words to posterity.

"Only he felt he could no more dissemble,
And kiss'd her, mouth to mouth, all of a tremble."
Leigh Hunt in 'The Story of Rimimi'

"For years she will recall the day,
When she walked down the aisle
With shining teardrop in her eye,
And on her lips a smile.
And in her heart she'll treasure still
That very happy day
When in the church before the guests
She gave herself away."
Marcia Dobson-Blythe in 'The Wedding Day'

"And now kind friends what I have wrote,
I hope you will pass o'er,
And not criticise as some have done
Hitherto herebefore."
Julia Moore in 'The Sweet Singer of Michigan'

"O Moon, when I gaze on thy beautiful face,
Careering along through the boundaries of space,
The thought has often come into my mind
If I ever shall see thy glorious behind."
quoted by Robert Ross in 'The Academy'

"Dust to dust, and ashes to ashes,
Into her tomb the Great Queen dashes."
'On the Death of Queen Victoria' by a Babu Poet

"Ah, lovely appearance of death!
What sight upon Earth is so fair?
Not all the gay pageants that breathe
Can with a dead body compare."
'On the Sight of a Corpse' by John Wesley

"The frog he sits upon the bank
And catches bugs and flies,
And after he gets tired of that
He just jumps in and dives."
James K Elmore

"A bad act lives forever.
A good one never dies,
But with this difference —
The one causes a beautiful sensation
To pass through the system
That makes this Earth a Heaven —
The other Hades."
Evan Llewellyn in 'Giddy Mary and other Poems'

"Backward the sun, an unknown motion went;
The stars gazed on, and wondered what he meant."
Abraham Cowley in 'Davideis'

"God has took their little treasure,
And his name I'll tell you now,
He had gone from earth forever
Their little Charles Henry House."
Julie Moore in 'Little Henry'

"I wandered lonely as a … cow?…no, what's the word?"

While eating dinner this dear child
Was choked on a piece of beef.
Doctors came, tried their skill awhile,
But none could give relief.
Her friends and schoolmates will not forget
Little Libbie that is no more;
She is waiting on the shining step,
To welcome home friends once more."

Julie Moore in 'Little Libbie'

"God prosper long our noble Queen,
    And long may she reign!
Maclean he tried to shoot her,
    But it was all in vain.
For God He turned the ball aside,
    Maclean aimed at her head;
And he felt very angry
    Because he didn't shoot her dead."

William McGonagall in
'Attempted Assassination of the Queen'

The poetry of Margaret Cavendish, Duchess of Newcastle, had the honour of being described by Samuel Pepys as "the most ridiculous thing that ever was wrote". This is her 'What is Liquid?':

"All that doth flow we cannot liquid name
Or else would fire and water be the same;
But that is liquid which is moist and wet
Fire that property can never get.
Then 'tis not cold that doth the fire put out
But 'tis the wet that makes it die, no doubt."

Many people consider 'A Tragedy', published in 1874 by the minor Pre-Raphaelite poet Theophilus Marzials, to be the worst poem ever written in the English language. Here is the first verse:

"Death!
  Plop.
The barges down in the river flop.
    Flop, plop.
    Above, beneath.
From the slimy branches the grey drips drop,
As they scraggle black on the thin grey sky,
Where the black cloud rack-hackles drizzle and fly
To the oozy waters, that lounge and flop
On the black scrag piles, where the loose cords plop,
As the raw wind whines in the thin tree-top."

Of course, even great poets had their off-days:

"My father's, mother's brother's deaths I pardon;
That's somewhat, sure; a mighty sum of murder
Of innocent and kindred blood struck off.
My prayers and penance shall discount for these,
And beg of Heaven to charge the bill to me."
          John Dryden in 'Don Sebastian'

"Poor little foal of an oppressèd race!
I love the languid patience of thy face:
And oft with gentle hand I give thee bread,
And clap thy ragged coat, and pat thy head.
But what thy dulled spirits hath dismayed,
That never thou dost sport along the glade?"
          Samuel Taylor Coleridge in 'To a Young Ass'

"And thus continuing, she said,
'I had a son, who many a day
Sailed on the sea; but he is dead;
In Denmark he was cast away;
And I have travelled far as Hull to see
What clothes he might have left, or other property'."
          William Wordsworth in 'The Sailor's Mother'

"For me are homelier tasks prepared,
To the stone table in my garden
The Squire is come, and, as I guess,
His little ruddy daughter Bess
With Harry the Churchwarden."

> William Wordsworth in 'Prologue to Peter Bell'

"The tall masts quiver'd as they lay afloat,
The temples and the people and the shore;
One drew a sharp knife thro' my tender throat
Slowly, — and nothing more."

> Alfred, Lord Tennyson in 'A Dream of Fair Women'

In his Preface to 'Don Juan', Byron selects Wordsworth's 'The Thorn' as perhaps the worst poem ever written in English.

The reason why a poet of such eminence as Wordswoth could produce such doggerel has been fiercely debated by students and academics. I recall my tutor at Leeds University concluding, tongue-in-cheek, that it might be due to the depressing scenery of the Lake District.

"And to the left, three yards beyond,
You see a little muddy pond
Of water — never dry.
I measured it from side to side:
'Twas four feet long, and three feet wide."

The last couplet made him such a laughing stock that Wordsworth rewrote it before including the poem in his collected works.

Byron's criticism seems to me rather like the kettle calling the pan black, for some of his own early verse could hardly be described as great poetry. This word-picture, written in rollicking metre, of a weeping sailor, his tears dropping into the heaving ocean, and the soldier bathing with tears his enemy's wounds, strikes one as rather ludicrous:

"The man doom'd to sail with the blast of the gale,
Through billows Atlantic to steer,
As he bends o'er the wave which may soon be his grave,
The green sparkles bright with a Tear.

The soldier braves death for a fanciful wreath
In Glory's romantic career;
But he raises the foe when in battle laid low,
And bathes every wound with a Tear."

Lord Byron in 'The Tear'

Of course Yorkshire has its share of fine poets — Ted Hughes, Simon Armitage, Helen Dunmore, Vernon Scannell and Tony Harrison to mention but a few.

Two little-known and eminently forgettable poets from my home county deserve a mention in this section as versifiers of incredibly bad verse.

Laurence Eusden was regarded by many as the most undeserving holder of the title of Poet Laureate. Eusden, son of the Rector of Spofforth, was elevated to this position in 1718 by the Lord Chancellor, the Duke of Newcastle, who took a shine to this little-known poet after he wrote some highly flattering verses penned on the peer's marriage.

Eusden was regarded by his contemporaries as a third-rate poet who never even managed to publish a book of his own verse. Alexander Pope, a much greater poet of the time, wrote:

"Eusden, a laurel'd Bard, by fortune rais'd
By very few was read, by fewer prais'd."

It is not surprising that few found merit in Eusden's verse when we read his doggerel. Here is part of the 'Ode', written to celebrate the birthday of King George I. In it, the great Julius Caesar, arriving on the shores of Britain, is informed by a druid bard that a great king, much greater than he, will one day rule the land:

> "Tho thy flatt'ring Minions tell thee,
> None shall rise who shall excel thee;
> In revolving Years, believe me,
> (Heroe! I will not deceive thee).
> From distant German Climes shall rise
> A Heroe, more, than Julius, Wise;
> More Good, more Prais'd, more truly Great,
> Courted to sway BRITANNIA's State."

Pope was possibly a little peeved at the appointment of Eusden as Poet Laureate, and wrote Eusden's epitaph in the 'Dunciad':

> "Knoe, Eusden thirsts no more for sack or praise
> He sleeps amongst the dull of ancient days."

Another equally lacklustre Poet Laureate was Alfred Austin, born in Headingley, and vilified in his lifetime for his snobbishness, arrogance, tastelessness and complete lack of poetic talent.

Austin believed himself to be a poet of great genius and was delighted to be appointed to the high office in 1896 after the death of Alfred Lord Tennyson. Greater poets of the time like Kipling and Swinburne were passed over, for it was said that they were out of favour with Queen Victoria. Austin was much more prolific than Eusden and wrote enough verses to fill twenty volumes. Despite his industry, he carried the reputation of being a mediocre poet, and was the subject of great derision and the target of mockery. Here are a few examples of his verse:

> "Where loud the blackbird cheers his bride
> By some umbrageous vicarage."

> "The homebound rustic counts his wage,
> The same last week, the same the next."
>   'The Village Church'

"At last, by favour of Almighty God,
With bellying sail the fathers made Cape Cod."
'The Pilgrim Fathers'

"Then I fling the fisherman's flaccid corpse
At the feet of the fisherman's wife."
'The Wind'

"Love, though an egotist, can deify
A vulgar fault, and drape the gross with grace."
'The Human Tragedy'

It has to be said, however, that some of his verse, though simple and sentimental, has a certain charm:

"Poor little mite with mottled breast,
Half-fledged, and fallen from the nest,
For whom this world hath just begun,
Who want to fly, yet scarce can run;
Why open wide your yellow beak?
Is it for hunger, or to speak —
To tell me that you fain would be
Loosed from my hand to liberty?"
'A Captive Throstle'

Austin was reputed to have written some of the worst poetry in the English language. It was alleged that when the Prince of Wales was ill, he wrote:

"Flash'd from his bed the electric tidings came,
He is no better, he is much the same."

It was also claimed that in celebrating the disastrous Jameson Raid in December/January 1895-6 he penned the lines:

"They went across the veldt
As hard as they could pelt."

In fact, as this correspondent wrote in his letter to the *Daily Telegraph* in March 2013, Alfred Austin was much maligned:

> "SIR — I am glad that, in your leading article, you did not join in the generally ignorant execration of Alfred Austin (1835-1913), the Poet Laureate.
>
> "The best-known couplet ascribed to him is in fact an anonymous parody supposedly on the subject of the sickness of the Prince of Wales in 1871:
>
>> "'Flash'd from his bed the electric tidings came,
>> He is no better, he is much the same.'
>
> "These lines were popularised by E F Benson, who preferred a good story to accuracy.
>
> "Nor did Austin write the jangling couplet said to occur in his first poem as Laureate, 'Jameson's Ride'. The mockers say it goes:
>
>> "'They went across the veldt,
>> As hard as they could pelt.'
>
> "The truth is not quite so bad:
>
>> "'So we forded and galloped forward,
>> As hard as our beasts could pelt,
>> First eastward, then tending northward,
>> Right over the rolling veldt.'
>
> "The job of Poets Laureate is hard enough without their being blamed for lines they did not write."

THE LAST WORD

Epitaphs and memorials

Of last words, none is more final than an epitaph: the definitive moment of self-congratulation; a last opportunity to commend oneself to the world and one's maker; or simply a chance to warn others of their impending fate. These often pithy statements about the lately departed, carved forever on a tombstone, can be simple or florid, boastful or modest, serious and poignant or witty and amusing.

The earliest epitaphs in English date from the Reformation. Prior to this time it was usual practice to have the simple phrase 'Pray for the soul of…' carved in the tombstone, but soon more elaborate words extolling the virtues of the deceased person were used.

Yorkshire, of course, has some cracking epitaphs. Perhaps the most famous is that of a former headmistress of Doncaster Girls' Grammar School who died in the 1920s. She had asked for the inscription "She was thine" to be carved on her headstone.

Unfortunately the apprentice stonemason given the task omitted the letter 'e' from 'thine', with the result that the inscription read: "She was thin". The stonemason, alerted to the error, duly told the apprentice to add the 'e'. It then read:

"E, she was thin."

There is an unusual twist to this unlikely but true story. The stone was discovered in a garage in Baltimore. Apparently for some bizarre reason it had been bequeathed to the second son of a member of the late headmistress's family.

Yorkshire graveyards abound with wonderful last words:

> Here I lie with my two daughters,
> Killed by taking the Harrogate waters.

> All you who care my grave to see,
> Avoid damp beds and think of me.

In Malton an inscription reads:

> Here lies the father of 29.
> It would have been more,
> But he didn't have time.

Another in All Saints' Church in Darfield, near Barnsley, states:

> The mortal remains of Robert Millthorp who died on
> September 13th 1826 aged 19 years. He lost his life by
> inadvertently throwing this stone upon himself whilst
> in the service of James Raywood of Ardsley, who erected
> it in his memory.

This gravestone erected by a 'grieving' widow has a sting:

> Under this sod lies another.

Epitaphs give a brief glimpse at another person's life. They are usually composed by those who, having lost a loved one, want to express the loss simply, sincerely and in a heartfelt way.

Occasionally an epitaph is a reminder that we all will one day join 'the Great Majority':

> All you good people
> That here pass by,

As you are now
So once was I.
As I am now,
You soon shall be.
Therefore prepare thyself
To follow me.

Young man prepare yourself to die,
For life is short and Death is nigh.
Prepare yourself, make no delay
For I in my prime was snatched away.

> Richard Wallis (1744-7)

All ye who stop to read this stone,
Ponder how soon she was gone.
Death doth not always warning give,
Therefore be careful how you live.

> Mary Richards (1740-1771),
> St Mary's Church, Doddington

Some epitaphs are witty reminders of the person's profession or pastimes in life:

Here lies poor but honest Bryan Tunstall.
He was a most expert Angler,
Until Death, envious of his merit,
Threw out His line, hooked him
And landed him here on the 21st day of April 1790.

Just as the leaves drop at the end of the year,
Gently he lies with his wife weeping near.
Gone is the fighter gone from the fray,
Gone is the actor gone from the play.
Homme d'esprit

> Charles Oglethorpe, actor manager

Stranger, tread this ground with
        Gravity
Dentist Brown is filling his last
        Cavity.
           tombstone in St George's Church, Edinburgh

Going, Going, Gone!
       John H Wells, auctioneer

Here lieth John Cruker, a maker of bellows,
His craft's master, and king of good fellows;
Yet when he came to the hour of his death,
He that made bellows could not make breath.
       John Cruker, bellows maker

The Defence Rests.
       Mason Thornbury, attorney at law

Sometimes epitaphs are written not so much as a memento to those that have passed away but as a tribute to the author:

Farewell, thou child of my right hand and joy;
My sin was too much hope of thee, lov'd boy,
Seven years thou wert lent to me and I thee pay
Exacted by thy fate on the just day.
O, could I lose all father, now. For why
Will man lament the state he should envy?
To have so soon scap'd World's and flesh's rage,
And, if no other misery, yet age?
Rest in soft peace and ask'd say here doth lie
Ben Jonson his best piece of poetrie.
For whose sake, henceforth, all his vows be such
As what he loves may never live too much.
       eldest son of Ben Jonson (sixteenth century)

Epitaphs can be amusing, sometimes unintentionally:

> Sacred to the memory of
> John MacFarlane,
> Drowned in the waters of the Leith
> By a few affectionate friends.

> Life is a jest and all things show it.
> He thought so once and now he knows it.
>> John Gay, eighteenth-century poet

> Here lies an honest lawyer
> That is Strange.
>> John Strange, barrister

> Here lies the body of Jessica Jones
> Who died of eating cherry stones.
> Her name was Smith; it was not Jones;
> But Jones was put to rhyme with Stones.

> Beneath this smooth stone
> By the bone of his bone
> Sleeps Master John Gill;
> By lies when alive this attorney did thrive,
> And now he lies dead he lies still.

> She lived with her husband of fifty years
> And died in the confident hope of a better life.
>> Alice Mary Johnson, 1883-1947

> Here lies a lewd fellow, who, while he drew breath,
> In the midst of his life was in quest of his death;
> Which he quickly obtained for it cost him his life,
> For being in bed with another man's wife.

> In loving memory of my beloved wife, Hester, the mother
> of Edward, Richard, Mark, Penelope, John, Henry,

Michael, Susan, Emily, Charlotte, Amelia, George, Hugh,
Hester, Christopher and Daniel. She was a great breeder
of pugs, a devoted mother and dear friend.

> nineteenth-century grave, Hemel Hempstead

Some have children, some have none;
Here lies the mother of twenty-one.

> Ann Jennings, nineteenth century

Blown upward
Out of sight
He sought the leak
By candlelight.

> gravestone in Collingbourne, Wiltshire

John Edwards who perished in a fire.
None could hold a candle to him.

Hanged by mistake.

> On George Higson's tombstone, Arizona, USA

He died in peace
His wife died first.

> inscription at Ilfracombe, Devon

Here lies my poor wife, much lamented,
She is happy and I am contented.

> eighteenth century

Here lies my dear wife, a slattern and a shrew.
If I said I regretted her, I should lie too.

> nineteenth century

Here lies the body of Martha Dias,
Who was always uneasy and not over-pious.
She lived to the age of threescore and ten,
And gave that to the worms she refused to the men.

Here lie the bones of Elizabeth Charlotte
Born a virgin, died a harlot.
She was aye a virgin at seventeen
A remarkable thing in Aberdeen.

After a short, difficult and useless life,
Here rests in the Lord
Robert Tweddle, 1735, aged 32.
gravestone in Haltwhistle, Northumberland

Sacred to the memory of
Captain Anthony Wedgwood,
Accidentally shot by his gamekeeper
Whilst out shooting.
"Well done thou good and faithful servant."

Erected to the memory of
John Philips
accidentally shot
as a mark of affection by
his own brother.

In memory of John Smith
Who met violent death near this spot
18 hundred & 42.
He was shot by his own pistol.
It was none of the new kind
But an old-fashioned brass barrel,
and of such is the Kingdom of Heaven.

Here lies the body of Charlotte Greer,
Whose mouth would stretch from ear to ear.
Be careful as you tread this sod
For if she gapes, you're gone, by God!
died in 1900

Here lies the body of Thomas Vernon,
The only surviving son of Admiral Vernon
Died 23rd of July, 1753.

Jonathan Grober
Died dead and sober,
Lord thy wonders never cease.

Here lies the body of Richard Hind,
Who was neither ingenious, sober, nor kind.
>nineteenth century

Here I lie and no wonder I'm dead
For the wheel of the wagon ran over my head.
>grave in churchyard at Prendergast, South Wales

In loving memory of Frank Stainer
Of Staffordshire
Who left us in peace, 2nd Feb 1910

He was man of friendly mien and was literally
the father of all the children in the parish.
>Rev Edward Coker, eighteenth century

Oscar Wilde once observed that 'Death is too important a matter to be taken seriously.' Of course some epitaphs were designed to bring a smile to the lips of those who read them:

When I am dead, I hope it may be said:
'His sins were scarlet, but his books were read.'
>Hilaire Belloc

Bust to dust,
Lashes to ashes.
>Marilyn Monroe

I told you I was ill!
>Spike Milligan

My epitaph, I thought, might be soulful, like the one inscribed around the fountain at the Petwood Hotel in Woodall Spa in memory of Princess Diana:

> Time is too short for those who wait,
> Too swift for those who fear.
> Time is too long for those who grieve,
> Too short for those who rejoice,
> But for those who love — Time is eternity.

"I would like something which expresses a profound thought or feeling," I told my wife when I raised the matter with her (my assumption being, of course, that I would go first).

"What about the one we saw in the graveyard at St John's Church in Bermuda when we visited our son and family, erected in memory of Princely Dorothy?

> "If tears could build a stairway,
> And memories a lane,
> I'd walk right up to heaven's gates
> And bring you home again."

She arched an eyebrow. "Perhaps you ought to have something short, to the point and typically Yorkshire," Christine suggested:

> Under this stone my husband doth lie
> He's now at peace and so am I.

'I SPEAK IN THE TONGUES OF MEN AND OF ANGELS'

The great exponents of the language

> "Have something to say and say it as clearly
> as you can. That is the only secret to style."
> **Matthew Arnold**

The English teacher who told his class that the best kind of writing has colourful vocabulary, vivid imagery, a variety of sentence structure and detailed descriptions, was wrong. Clear, simple, plain and unambiguous English makes for the very best kind of writing. It should, like the works of the great writers, be easy to read and easy to listen to, and it exists in one timeless, ageless universe, fulfilling the requirements as stated in the *Quarterly Review* of 1844:

> "Good writing is the union of the highest art
> with the simplest form."

And there are so many examples of this: the Psalms of David, the Parables of Jesus, *Morte d'Arthur*, *Wuthering Heights*, *Pride and Prejudice*, *The Wind in the Willows*, *The Pilgrim's Progress*, *Gulliver's Travels*, *Adventures of Huckleberry Finn*, the works of Aldous Huxley and C S Lewis, E B White and Lewis Carroll, Charles Dickens and Jane Austen, Robert Louis Stevenson and Alan Bennett, and the poetry of Blake and Heaney, John Clare and W B Yeats. This is just a scratch on the surface of great English Literature.

So finally allow me just a few personal choices which show the skill and pervasiveness of language, the power and emotive strength of the printed word to stir the imagination of the reader.

> If I speak in the tongues of men and of angels, but have not love, I am a noisy gong or a clanging cymbal. And if I have prophetic powers, and understand all mysteries and all knowledge, and if I have all faith, so as to remove mountains, but have not love, I am nothing. If I give away all I have, and if I deliver up my body to be burned, but have not love, I gain nothing.
>
> Love is patient and kind; love does not envy or boast; it is not arrogant or rude. It does not insist on its own way; it is not irritable or resentful; it does not rejoice at wrong-doing, but rejoices with the truth. Love bears all things, believes all things, hopes all things, endures all things.
>
> Love never ends. As for prophecies, they will pass away; as for tongues, they will cease; as for knowledge, it will pass away. For we know in part and we prophesy in part, but when the perfect comes, the partial will pass away.
>
> When I was a child, I spoke like a child, I thought like a child, I reasoned like a child. When I became a man, I gave up childish ways. For now we see in a mirror dimly, but then face to face. Now I know in part; then I shall know fully, even as I have been fully known.
>
> So now faith, hope, and love abide, these three; but the greatest of these is love.
>
> First Epistle to the Corinthians, chapter 13

She should have died hereafter;
There would have been a time for such a word.
To-morrow, and to-morrow, and to-morrow,
Creeps in this petty pace from day to day
To the last syllable of recorded time,

And all our yesterdays have lighted fools
The way to dusty death. Out, out, brief candle!
Life's but a walking shadow, a poor player
That struts and frets his hour upon the stage
And then is heard no more: it is a tale
Told by an idiot, full of sound and fury,
Signifying nothing.

William Shakespeare, *Macbeth*, Act 5 Scene 5

Tread lightly, she is near
Under the snow,
Speak gently, she can hear
The daisies grow.

All her bright golden hair
Tarnished with rust,
She that was young and fair
Fallen to dust.

Lily-like, white as snow,
She hardly knew
She was a woman, so
Sweetly she grew.

Coffin-board, heavy stone,
Lie on her breast,
I vex my heart alone,
She is at rest.

Peace, peace, she cannot hear
Lyre or sonnet,
All my life's buried here,
Heap earth upon it.

Oscar Wilde, 'Requiescat'

'The Tyger' is perhaps the most famous of William Blake's lyric poems. First published in 1794 in *Songs of Experience*, its apparent simplicity makes it appealing to children, while its religious, political and mythological imagery provokes endless debate amongst scholars. Whatever the case, it remains as one of the most evocative pieces of poetry in the English language.

Tyger! Tyger! burning bright
In the forests of the night,
What immortal hand or eye
Could frame thy fearful symmetry?

In what distant deeps or skies
Burnt the fire of thine eyes?
On what wings dare he aspire?
What the hand dare seize the fire?

And what shoulder, & what art.
Could twist the sinews of thy heart?
And when thy heart began to beat,
What dread hand? & what dread feet?

What the hammer? what the chain?
In what furnace was thy brain?
What the anvil? what dread grasp
Dare its deadly terrors clasp?

When the stars threw down their spears,
And watered heaven with their tears,
Did he smile his work to see?
Did he who made the Lamb make thee?

Tyger! Tyger! burning bright
In the forests of the night,
What immortal hand or eye
Dare frame thy fearful symmetry?

The virtues of humility and charity are at the centre of the Christian faith, and these quatrains reflect those sentiments:

> Humble we must be, if to heaven we go:
> High is the roof there; but the gate is low.
> Whene'r thou speak'st, look with a lowly eye:
> Grace is increased by humility.
>> Robert Herrick, 1591-1674

> Be you to others kind and true,
> As you'd have others be to you;
> And neither do nor say to men
> Whate'er you would not take again.
>> Isaac Watts, 1674-1748

In the sonnet 'Death Be Not Proud' by John Donne (1572-1631), death is depicted as a person, and the poem is a fine example of personification. At the time it was believed that the wicked and unrepentant would go to the everlasting flames of hell; here the poet makes the concept less alarming and mysterious.

> Death be not proud, though some have called thee
> Mighty and dreadfull, for, thou art not soe,
> For, those, whom thou think'st, thou dost overthrow,
> Die not, poore death, nor yet canst thou kill mee.
> From rest and sleepe, which but thy pictures bee,
> Much pleasure, then from thee, much more must flow,
> And soonest our best men with thee doe goe,
> Rest of their bones, and soules deliverie.
> Thou art slave to Fate, Chance, kings, and desperate men,
> And dost with poyson, warre, and sicknesse dwell,
> And poppie, or charmes can make us sleepe as well,
> And better then thy stroake; why swell'st thou then?
> One short sleepe past, wee wake eternally,
> And death shall be no more; death, thou shalt die.

The Pilgrim's Progress from This World to That Which Is to Come (1678) is a Christian allegory by John Bunyan, and is universally admired for its simplicity, vigour and beauty of language.

Then Christian began to gird up his loins, and to address himself to his journey. So the other told him that, by that he was gone some distance from the gate he would come to the house of the Interpreter, at whose door he should knock, and he would show him excellent things. Then Christian took his leave of his friend, and he again bid him God-speed. Then he went on till he came at the house of the Interpreter, where he knocked over and over. At last one came to the door, and asked who was there.

CHRISTIAN. Sir, here is a traveller, who was bid by an acquaintance of the good man of this house to call here for my profit; I would therefore speak with the master of the house.

So he called for the master of the house, who, after a little time, came to Christian, and asked him what he would have.

CHRISTIAN. Sir, said Christian, I am a man that am come from the City of Destruction, and am going to the Mount Zion; and I was told by the man that stands at the gate at the head of this way, that if I called here you would show me excellent things, such as would be helpful to me on my journey.

INTERPRETER. Then said Interpreter, Come in; I will show thee that which will be profitable to thee. So he commanded his man to light the candle, and bid Christian follow him. So he had him into a private room, and bid his man open a door; the which, when he had done, Christian saw the picture a very grave person hang up against the wall; and this was the fashion of it; it had eyes lifted up to heaven, the best of books in its hand, the law of truth was written upon its lips, the world was behind its back; it stood as if it pleaded with men, and a crown of gold did hang over its head.

CHRISTIAN. Then said Christian, What meaneth this?

INTERPRETER. The man whose picture this is, is one of a thousand: he can beget children, (1 Cor. iv. 15), travail in birth with children, (Gal. iv. 19), and nurse them himself when they are born. And whereas, thou seest him with his eyes lift up to heaven, the best of books in his hand, and the law of truth writ on his lips: it is to show thee, that his work is to know, and unfold dark things to sinners; even as also thou seest him stand as if he pleaded with men. And whereas thou seest the world as cast behind him, and that a crown hangs over his head: that is to show thee, that, slighting and despising the things that are present, for the love that he hath to his Master's service, he is sure, in the world that comes next, to have glory for his reward. Now, said the Interpreter, I have showed thee this picture first, because the man whose picture this is, is the only man whom the Lord of the place whither thou art going, hath authorised to be thy guide in all difficult places thou mayest meet with in the way. Wherefore take good heed to what I have showed thee, and bear well in thy mind what thou hast seen, lest in thy journey thou meet with some that pretend to lead thee right - but their way goes down to death.

Barchester Towers by Anthony Trollope is wonderfully humorous, both in the dialogue of the characters and in the novelist's third-person narration. Trollope's humour is in the wordplay and hyperbole. For example, when the awkward and unattractive Mr Obadiah Slope, the bishop's ambitious, unctuous and wheedling chaplain, is soon to declare his love for the beautiful Signora Neroni, he takes her hand:

> Mr Slope was big, awkward, cumbrous, and having his heart in his pursuit, was ill at ease. The lady was fair, as we have said, and delicate; everything about her was fine and refined; her hand in his looked like a rose lying among carrots, and when he kissed it he looked as a cow might do on finding such a flower among her food.

Winston Churchill's speech in the House of Commons on 4th June 1940 is surely one of Churchill's finest oratorical moments. It surges with pride and defiance. In the sentence ending in 'surrender' only the last word — surrender — does not have Old English roots.

It is said that as the House of Commons thundered in an uproar at his stirring rhetoric, Churchill muttered in a whispered aside to a colleague:

"And we'll fight them with the butt ends of broken beer bottles because that's bloody well all we've got!"

> Even though large tracts of Europe and many old and famous states have fallen or may fall into the grip of the Gestapo and all the odious apparatus of Nazi rule, we shall not flag or fail. We shall go on to the end. We shall fight in France, we shall fight on the seas and oceans, we shall fight with growing confidence and growing strength in the air, we shall defend our island, whatever the cost may be. We shall fight on the beaches, we shall fight on the landing grounds, we shall fight in the fields and in the streets, we shall fight in the hills; we shall never surrender. And if, which I do not for a moment believe, this island or a large part of it were subjugated and starving, then our Empire beyond the seas, armed and guarded by the British Fleet, would carry on the struggle, until, in God's good time, the New World, with all its power and might, steps forth to the rescue and the liberation of the old.

AND FINALLY...

Pythagoras' Theorem	24 words
The Lord's Prayer	66 words
Archimedes Principle	67 words
The Ten Commandments	179 words
The American Declaration of Independence	1,300 words
European Union Regulation on the sale of cabbages	26,911 words